SELF LIBERATION FOR THE MELANATED PEOPLE

By

Bro. Lyle

Published 2021 by Melanated Global Publishing House LLC.

Acknowledgement

First and foremost, I would like to give praises to The Universal ALL, who is the Alpha and Omega of all existence. Secondly, I would like to thank my beautiful Queen; lovely children; wonderful mother; and sister who give me that extra motivation to keep striving towards success. As a student of scholarly study, I must give thanks to these great scholars who came before me; Dr. John Henrik Clarke, Dr. Yosef Ben Jochannan, Dr. Leonard Jeffries, Dr. Ray Hagins, Prof. Kaba Hiawatha Kamene, Prof. Cheikh Anta Diop, Ivan Van Sertima, Bobby Hemmitt, Bro. Tracy Barney, Allen J. Z. Shabazz, Anthony T. Browder, the Late Great Marcus Garvey, and the Late Great Honorable Malcolm X. These esteemed Elders helped to shape my perception of Self Liberation in the most unimaginable way.

This book is dedicated to my late Father Bro. Lyle Sr.

(11/13/1961 - 03/20/2016)

I would also like to thank Katia Herrera for creating such a masterful artwork for this book cover. Katia can be reached at society6.com/creativepowerr for all your afrocentric artistic needs.

Introduction

"We can never CHANGE the past; but we can always REVOLUTIONIZE the future…" -Bro. Lyle

It is with great honor that I present this profound body of work. Over the past 500 plus years the melanated people have been suffering from historical systematic oppression in the diaspora of the Americas. There's also a narrative that suggests melanated people have never contributed anything historically great to civilization throughout the world. My goal is to help stimulate the mental process of my people in order to liberate themselves from the psychological brainwashing which has been placed upon them. "Self Liberation For The Melanated People", is structured as a step by step guide with the feeling of a personal conversation between you and the author. Each chapter in this literature is broken up into several sub-topics for deeper understanding while synthesizing its way philosophically.

First, we will cover the topic of "Self-Love", because love for self must be implemented before any thought of liberation. Self-love provides the very first building block for any existing aspirations in one's life. The very moment you face yourself in the mirror, there should be a certain level of love, pride, and acceptance. Secondly, we will break down the true essence of liberation in its entirety. Knowing the construct of the idea will help you better understand what is needed to obtain liberation. The concept of liberation at its early stages has to be intersected with "Knowledge of Self". Without self-knowledge, he or she could never appreciate their ancestral greatness, therefore, leaving them to accept any stigma placed upon them. Knowledge of Self also deals with understanding your personal spirituality because we must become aligned with our inner-self in order to become conscious. Next, you will have to "Regain Self Awareness" by understanding what "Cultural Imperialism" has done to the melanated community. Every society who has ever been invaded or sold into slavery have delt with deculturalization in one form or another. Revisiting and uncovering the root of stolen cultures is imperative for those who wish to change the narrative of today's conditions.

After unveiling hidden truths of our culture, we then can educate ourselves on financial literacy. Black economics will undoubtedly have a major impact on rebuilding the melanated communities. There has been a major mis-educational process in dealing with how money works; exploitation of communities; and the power of credit. Once a certain level of knowledge is obtained, we can incorporate all resources that's necessary to move forward.

In addition to those topics mentioned, there will be loads of ancient and modern scholarly inserts. You will read philosophies from the Ancient Hermetic Texts, Marcus Garvey, Malcolm X, Pro. Kaba Kamene and many more. There's also a great deal of historical facts that are not being taught in Western society school systems such as ancient civilizations, great warriors, and inventions that are also documented. Spirituality and metaphysical concepts will also gracefully flow through these pages while igniting an awakening within. So set back, grab a cup of coffee; a glass of wine; or your favorite choice of tea; and enjoy this profound work of literature. Much Love, Peace, and Blessings.

-Bro. Lyle

Table of Contents

Dr. Martin Luther King Jr.

Dr. Ray Hagins

Prof. Kaba Hiawatha Kamene

Jay Morrison

Cheikh Anta Diop

Bob Marley

James Baldwin

Thomas Sankara

Frederick Douglass

Bro. Lyle

"The Formula"

When examining any situation which needs to be dissected, there must be a systematic formula at hand. With that statement understood, I decided to create a very simple formula that can be used to decipher the ongoing situation centering the lack of mental liberation amongst the melanated people globally. We must understand the fundamental psychological aspects of hidden properties that manipulate our position in society. This is why I came up with the **FORMULA:** (Self-love + Knowledge Of Self + Financial Literacy = Self Liberation).

Everything in life deals with a formulated structure. We can observe successful companies that started from ground zero and ascended towards prosperity. Those companies had some sort of formula that included budgeting, marketing, and people relations in order to succeed. There're also chemical formulas that we use in everyday life that involve cooking (recipe), medicine (pharmacist), cleaning supplies etc. Everywhere you look there's a formula used to achieve a specific goal. I can go on and on with different examples, but I'm sure my point is made. Therefore, it's important for us to strategize a way to gain leverage in today's society so that liberation will become the new "normal".

<u>Self-love -</u> is when a person accepts every physical, emotional, and spiritual essence of themself. Self-love is the first building block needed for a foundational structure towards liberation. You must sincerely LOVE and cherish every aspect of your EXISTENCE unapologetically. If you have no love for self, the thought of liberation is pretty much invalid.

<u>Knowledge of Self -</u> is when a person truly knows themself. You have to know your true **history,** not **"his-story".** When the invader tells **his-story "my-story"** becomes a **[mystery]** . Before you go further, re-read those last plays on words for clarity. We must also realize the importance of knowing the inner spiritual aspect of one's self as well. To embody your spiritual essence, you must align yourself with the universe from which you came. This can be done by meditating; proper dieting; and studying nature itself. These are the keys to opening doors to your higher self.

<u>Financial Literacy -</u> is actually understanding how money works and how to use resources to build up communities. Most melanated families weren't taught about ownership or the trickery of exploitation in their neighborhoods. Financial literacy is just as important as any other ideology that I will ever mention. We must control the economic structures in our local communities first and foremost. The days of foreigners owning everything must come to an end if we wish to excel as a people. With that in mind, it's imperative that we teach ownershgip; the value of credit; and **UNITY!!!**

These are the 3 steps I formulated together in hopes of gaining **Self-liberation** as a people. As you continue to submerge yourself in the pages of this profound body of literature, you will uncover countless amounts of informational **TRUTH.** Let's build and re-establish our situation. -Bro. Lyle

Chapter I

SELF LOVE

"Self-love is a Divine principle; it deals with your spirituality; mental state; and physical care. You have to LOVE & cherish each aspect of your EXISTENCE" -Bro Lyle

Before your mind can be fixated around self-liberation you must first gain self-love. Love for self should always be a measure of natural consciousness. Without this awareness you can easily be manipulated into thinking less of yourself. Then as time passes by it will become almost impossible to understand your worth and purpose in life.

When dealing with reality, true fulfillment comes from not worrying about what others perceive of you. Why should you have to generate thousands of likes, hearts, and comments on social media platforms just to feel whole? Furthermore, why should you have to compete with co-workers, classmates, church members, and political leaders to feel accomplished or empowered over others in the community? There are too many of us in this generation that are starving for what is already inside of us from birth. Each and everyone of us are blessed with a meaningful purpose in life at the very moment we were born. Your race, gender, or financial background will never dictate how special your purpose is. During a point in time, we must find our inner sense of being. Trying to figure out self purpose is absurd without self love because it is the original building block to all liberation. You will be mentally doomed from the beginning if this process is not aligned with your true self. I encourage you to dig deep within your souls, spirits, hearts and minds in order to find that **SELF-LOVE.**

<u>Part 1. To the Man</u>

My fellow man, look at yourself head on in the mirror. Take off that expensive high end bezzled wristwatch. Remove that iced out cubanlink chain from around your neck. For the extra cool type brothers, remove them Ray-Ban shades from your face. Now take that house note Gucci outfit off and put some cheap department store sweats on. If you're a gym rat it's cool but lay off the flexing just for a short moment. Make a quick phone call to your crazy shellshocked uncle and trade him your new Cadillac Escalade for his old rusty 91' Chevy truck just for the weekend. How do you feel with this new appearance? Do you feel like a bare soul with no leverage on life all a sudden? Are you shaking your head with disgust viewing yourself as lame? Is there a huge void inside that emulates the black hole of the cosmos? Think about those questions with patients and honesty.

Viewing those questions with honest intent should have brought you to a certain mind frame. Can you see a King who needs no validation? Will the very essence of your being overthrow any superficial illusions of modern society? Creating your own footprints in the sand will undoubtedly define your true character. The world we reside in will try its hardest to drain every ounce of spiritual awareness that you possess within, but it's your duty to stay firm.

Man must sincerely grasp the acknowledgment of knowing his true purpose. Having the most money, biggest house, or finest car, has nothing to do with true fulfillment. I can't express this sentiment enough. Earthly gains are only momentary achievements for the physical form. Keep in mind that health is true wealth ultimately by any measure. To be clear, prosperity should not be frowned upon because poverty is the last situation a person would want to find themselves in. Financial freedom and independence should always be a top priority in order to support one's family. I'm only suggesting that we have to be careful not to lose sight of what really matters in life. Dating back to recent history you can find wealthy people who were so hurt over stock market crashes and failed business ventures, they decided to commit suicide to escape reality. That alone should inspire love for self above all. Relying on a financial status cannot carry you through all phases of life. Substance and virtue must be prevalent at all times.

The melanated man must also understand that he is a King by divine order. Becoming the King of your own domain spiritually, must be reached before any form of leadership. Everybody wants to wear the crown without taking proper steps to gain the wisdom that's necessary. Educating yourself on spirituality, economics and self care is essential. With all that has been mentioned, a King cannot forget the importance of his beloved Queen. Miraculously, the Creator has blessed us with a Queen who yearns to be the backbone of her King. Not to place her underneath in any way, instead it is to exemplify her importance. She is to be treated with the highest of esteem and respect. Every great empire had that gracious Queen who helped to keep stability within its union. The man and woman must always work in unison. Nature actually teaches the importance of all male and female conjunctions. Let me explain this concept for a brief moment. All aspects of life deal with male and female unity which can be observed in everyday life. The key (male) has to insert the ignition port (female) in order to start the vehicle. The electric plug (m) has to insert the wall outlet (fm) to receive an electric charge. Even the door jams and locks have a male and female principle. Studying nature alone is all that's needed to understand the importance of the male and female to one another.

A man's presence also deals with initial impressions when presenting himself in public. The way a man conducts himself determines the level of respect he generates from others; "like it or not." Confidence and high character is the perfect combination for receiving positive energies during physical encounters. Your dress attire should also be in accordance with your representation. Too many times I see our brothers walk around in public showing the world what type of underwear they have on. In most situations he has to walk with one hand holding the waist or belt while attempting to balance his poster. Tell me how does it make any sense to struggle with your clothing while simply buying the proper size would be more sufficient. Judging my people is not the objective because I once was at that same place in life. Advocating self respect for our young Kings is my only concern. Teaching them to properly show self-respect for themselves has to be addressed in today's society.

We as men must contribute more to our households as well. There are way too many one parent homes in the melanated communities. Young boys in particular who are raised without their fathers are most likely to venture out in the streets for guidance. When the dopeman, gang member, and thief is the role model for our sons, how can we expect positive futures for them? It's in our hands to do whatever it takes to properly groom them into manhood. I understand that sometimes the mother and father may not be together, but co-parenting must be established. Time is so precious in the developmental stages of a child and it passes with a blink of an eye. The system is angled to destroy the black communities in America, so changing the narrative mustn't go undone.

Part 2. To the Woman

My dear sisters, look in the mirror at yourself head on and wash off that caked up makeup that's on your beautiful faces. Relax every muscle in your face while staring with a blank demeanor. Now cut out all those hair extensions (weave) that's sewed into your natural hair. Afterwards, wash out all those damaging chemicals from your hair follicles. As you focus on your body, take off that waist trainer which is squeezing the life out of you! Then replace those exotic lace panties with some boring cotton underwear. At this moment, please stop sucking your stomach in and finally exhale! Turn away from your favorite side and face yourself forward in pure honesty. Analyze and know that at this moment you're gazing at The Creator's perfect creation. With all humility tell me what do you see?

Is there a certain level of disappointment in sight when you no longer are draped in superficial beauty? Would you rather turn the lights off, climb in bed, and lay under covers with tears of pity? Do you wish The Creator had constructed your appearance into a totally different ethnic group with contrasting features from yours? On the other hand, are you seeing a comforting version of natural beauty? Observing this new found beauty should bring forth a sense of pride. Let it all set in for a moment.

Women have been the quintessential essence of the word beauty since the first sunrise of existence. There's not one waterfall, landscape, sunrise, sunset, ruby, or diamond that compares to a woman's beauty. With that said, the term beauty does not only speak to her physicality, but also to her sensuality. Sensuality comes from the root word sensual. Sensual is defined as receiving arousing gratification to your senses but not necessarily sexually. Her warm touch can melt the coldest of hearts.

The sweet charisma she possesses could turn you against your own better judgement. She is special in every way imaginable.

The Creator has also blessed the woman with perhaps the most special gift known to man called the womb. My views aligned this gift with being Godlike ideally speaking. Let me break this down for you. The womb coincides with creation at its purest form. Childbirth is nature's most wonderful miracle. Duplicating human creation which carries a soul is impossible any other way. Through this process she has helped to bring forth endless amounts of perfectly imperfect generations of humanity.

The Late Great Muhamad Ali once had a conversation with his daughter about self-dignity and respect. The following account took place when Ali's daughter arrived at his home wearing inappropriate clothing. Here is the story told by one of his daughters from the book ("*More than a Hero:* Muhammad Ali's Life Lessons through his daughter's eyes")

"When we finally arrived, the chauffeur escorted my younger sister, Laila, and I up to my father's suite. As usual he was hiding behind the door to scare us. We exchanged many hugs and kisses as we could possibly give in one day. My father took a good look at us. Then he sat

me down on his lap and said something that I will never forget. He looked me straight in the eyes and said "Hana, everything that God made valuable in the world is covered and hard to get to. Where do you find diamonds? Deep down in the ground covered and protected. Where do you find pearls? Deep down in the bottom of the ocean covered up and protected in a beautiful shell. Where do you find gold? Way down in the mine covered over with layers and layers of rocks. You've got to work hard to get to them!'' He looked at me with serious eyes, "Your body is sacred. You're far more precious than diamonds and pearls and you should be covered too.''

Bro. Muhammad Ali knew the essential value of the woman. It was expressed through his personal philosophies that the woman is the most precious element on Earth and should conduct herself as such. Women are obligated to hold themself to a high standard because it exemplifies true self love.

Please don't take me addressing the above topic as negative. In my opinion, modeling for an athletic swimsuit line or lingerie is not degrading long as it's on a professional level. My concern is when our Queens dress half naked in public while searching for attention. A man will view her in a certain light if she refuses to show self-respect. Calling her out her name or even grabbing at her isn't uncommon if he has no respect for her. My dear Queens must demand respect at all cost by first implementing self-love and self-respect. Nothing is wrong with buying your outfits as long as it's appropriate. Catch that eye contact with a certain individual if you must, but please hold your morals at its highest of esteems. By doing so, your daughters will follow by example and we would have fewer young ladies exposing themselves inappropriately. The teenage pregnancy rate would start to decline because everyone would have a greater appreciation for self instead of hoping for acceptance.

All women are encouraged to accept their God given worth. Never let anyone degrade you! Know you are a Queen in your own right. Beauty is measured inside as well as on the outside but the former is most important. Remember that nothing is wrong with makeup or hair extensions, but never convince yourself that you are not beautiful without them. Love yourself unconditionally by all means for it is imperative. This is my message to the woman.

"We must embrace our natural essence in order to move forward...You are Powerful; Organic; Unique; and Divine...Ase'... " -Bro. Lyle

Masculine and Feminine ENERGY

In addition to understanding the importance of self-love, we must also learn how to balance our **energy/frequency** levels. Both male and female have specific qualities that permeate through their essence. These are qualities that distinguish the difference between the two. Thus, we must be conscious enough to realize that both male and female share each other's respected qualities, but to different degrees. I will share a few simple developmental strategies that you can use for healthy energy developing.

Masculine Energy

- Be precise and confident in your expressions

- Be firm while setting your boundaries

- Set daily goals that you know can be accomplished

- Cultivate your inner peace at all cost

- Be conscious with your sexual energy

- Be the protector of your home and family

Feminine Energy

- Listen to your intuitions at all cost

- Be the nurturer that you are intended to be

- Always speak up on what you feel

- Find strength in your sensitivity

- Cultivate openness with your relationships

- Embrace the essence of "being"

The "Principle of Gender", from the 7 Hermetic Principles, teaches us how every emanation from creation has a male and female principle which works in unison. So, once we master our respected divine masculine or feminine energy; we must then master our counterpart's energy as well. Once this is accomplished, then you will have complete mastery over self.

Chapter II. Explaining Liberation

"Liberate the minds of men and ultimately you will liberate the bodies of men…" -Marcus Garvey

Part 1. Definition of Liberation

In chapter one we discussed the importance of having self-love first and foremost. It's understood that self-love is the first step to developing a mental concept for liberation. Gaining a structural understanding of liberation has to be done with calculated steps. Now I will break down liberation's **definition** and the critical parts that correspond with the idea. This chapter is formulated as a brief review from a **definitional** standpoint. I will give a more thorough examination of what needs to be done to achieve liberation as we read further into this book.

Self liberation can be defined as the act or process of freeing someone or something from another's control; the act of liberating someone or something.

My views of self-liberation are also as follows:

A.) To cancel out all mental oppressive ideas that have been implemented in the minds of the oppressed. **Example:** If the invader or oppressor teaches the oppressed that he has no contribution to society in history and that his future will continue on the same trajectory; one has to take it upon himself to research the true history of his own roots in order to know thyself.

B.) To be freed of mental slavery. **Example:** You have to throw out the idea that your current state will never get better. Stop using oppression as a crutch to stay idle.

C.) The understanding that Cultural Imperialism is a way to create generational mind control. Cultural Imperialism happens when an invader comes to a civilization and strips the people of their culture, customs, and spirituality. After doing so, those invaders then implement their foreign customs onto the people mainly by force.

D.) To liberate you must also look back in your true history for the initial problem of your current state. You cannot expect to reverse a negative situation without first understanding the root of the problem.

"Emancipate yourself from mental slavery none but ourselves can free our minds, have no fear for atomic energy cause none of them can stop the time." -Bob Marley

Our minds are so fragile yet extremely powerful. Taking the stance to liberate from oppression is essential. As melanated people we cannot continue to walk around this diaspora in a sleep state. The Creator of all has blessed us with accessible knowledge in abundance. Unlike our ancestors, we now have millions of documented information available at the click of a finger. The internet is a magnificent tool that can be accessed anywhere. In the 20th century most of our scholars had to collect many books and encyclopedias in order to do research. If they wanted to travel the world they had to literally board a plane or boat to explore. Now we have the world wide web which can bring you to any place on the globe with a simple search request. Don't get me wrong; I for one, genuinely love reading books and collecting them for my personal library. I'm simply shedding light on the degree of accessible information which can be obtained. I remember talking to one of my mentors Bro. Tracy B., and he would always tell me how he had to sit down at his mother's kitchen table with multiple books and study for hours at a time. He reminds me how blessed this new generation is to have such easy access to infinite knowledge. With this immense degree of opportunity it is impossible to be left in the dark from information if you truly desire to learn.

There was an old saying, "If you want to hide something from a black man put it in a book". That phrase never set well with me in all my years as a youth. I always took those words personal because of the stereotypical implication. During my young adult years, I made sure to research any topic that interested me for better understanding. Research and learned knowledge gave me a sense of validation. It opened my eyes to a new level of awakening which only comes from pure determination. This is why I made it my personal mission to encourage each and every one to take advantage of available information. Having knowledge serves as life support for those who value substance.

"The liberation of the African mind, body, and spirit can only be achieved through the use of an African centered value system that makes the study of the success and failures of the past the highest priority..."

-Anthony T. Browder

"In order for Black people to understand the nature of the world they live in, they must first understand the nature or the people who interpreted the world for them…" -Anthony T. Browder

Part 2. Liberation through Proper Education

If life was depicted as an illustrated pyramid education would be at its peak. The old saying, "knowledge is power" still reigns supreme over ALL. Honestly speaking, there are people who wish to stay ignorant to this fact. In order for you to gain any sort of liberation you must first educate yourself on all facets of past, current, and future conditions. Lack of knowledge will only lead you to a continuous carousel of unsatisfied results.

We all know that melanated people suffer from social injustice; economic miseducation; lost knowledge of self; and racism. With this understanding, we must take proper steps towards rectifying these misfortunes. Once we familiarize ourselves on how to attack those problems, we must organize and then take action.

- **Social Injustice** is when one group of people within a society receives unfair treatment particularly when dealing with laws and legislations. Examples are: Voting Laws, Policing Laws, Environmental Laws, Health Care Laws, Education Laws, and Labor Laws. To change these problems, we must assemble a formulated agenda and organize calculated steps to change the legislation.

- **Economic Miseducation** is the lack of knowledge concerning the production, consumption, and transfer of wealth. With a plethora of websites, YouTube channels, business classes, and seminars that are available, we have unlimited access to financial knowledge. Most of us really can't afford to actually attend a university, so I highly recommend using these tools to educate yourself.

- **Lost Knowledge Of Self** is when you have no idea of the greatness from which you came. When you think your ancestors never contributed anything significant to society, then you my friend, lack "Knowledge of Self." Doing historical research and embodying the greatness of your ancestors will enlighten you to have an unbreakable sense of pride within.

- **Racism is**............. well you know.

Part 3. Liberation through Proper Diet

A proper diet that is filled with organic foods (mostly plant based) should be implemented in every household. It's no secret that most melanated people in the diaspora suffer from health issues due to poor dieting. Melanated people have a higher rate of diabetes, high cholesterol, and high blood pressure in the U.S. We are accustomed to eating foods that have higher salt and sugar properties. Fried chicken, ham-hocks, pork-chops, and boiled crawfish may taste like heaven to us, but it's a main contributor to the problem. In antiquity the majority of our ancestors consumed plant based foods from the earth. Many of those societies condemned the eating of several meats, which we can note in certain religious texts.

Western society teaches us that we need to eat meat in order to receive the correct amount of protein for our bodies. In contrast to Western society, science shows us that enzymes have to initially break down the meat in order for the body to receive protein. Why should you have to use a "middle man" to get to the protein when plant based foods produce a sufficient amount of protein in itself? I always tell people to study nature because it teaches everything there is to know. You have the gorilla, elephant, and oxen who survive off of vegetation. Each one of those mammals are very powerful and obviously have minimal problems with nutrition inefficiencies. We have to understand that processed meats and GMO products are a "BIG" business in this society that we live in.

Rates of High Blood Pressure by Race

- A greater percent of men (47%) have high blood pressure than women (43%)

- High blood pressure is more common in Melanated adults (54%) than in White adults (46%), Asian adults (39%), or Hispanic adults (36%).

- Blood pressure control by medicine is higher in White adults (32%) than in Melanated adults (25%), Hispanic adults (25%), and Asian adults (19%)

As the Original People of the planet, we must develop a diet that counters the toxic effects of western eating habits which causes infection and diseases. Clarity of thought, emotional balance, and awareness is also manifested from eating the proper foods that nature grows for us. Some may not know, but there is also a frequency that vibrates from these foods that will clear the body's energy channels, sustain immunity, vitality, and create longevity. Once you've changed your diet the mind, body, and spirit will begin to experience a higher level awakening within.

Part 4. Liberation through Meditation

"Wisdom relies on the single -mindedness of meditation, and meditation depends upon the self-awareness of morality." -Dalai Lama

Types of Meditation

1.) Two basic types of meditation are **analytical meditation and stabilizing meditation**. In analytical meditation you analyze a topic trying to understand it through reasoning. For instance, you might meditate on why things are impermanent by reflecting on how they are produced by causes or how they disintegrate moment by moment. In stabilizing meditation, you fix your mind on a single object or topic, such as impermanence. (Calm abiding is cultivated through stabilizing meditation.)

2.) Another way of dividing meditation is between **subjective meditation and objective meditation.** In subjective meditation your aim is to cultivate in the mind a new, or strengthened perspective, or attitude. The cultivation of faith is an example of this type of meditation; faith is not the object on which you are concentrating but an attitude that is being meditatively cultivated. (Cultivation of compassion is subjective meditation because you are not meditating on compassion but seeking to make your consciousness more compassionate.) In objective meditation you meditate on a topic, such as on impermanence.

3.) You can meditate in the manner of wishing. For example, you might wish to be filled with compassion, wisdom or psychic intuitions.

4.) You can go one step further into **imaginative meditation,** in which you can envision having qualities that you actually do not possess at the moment.

The act of meditating is a very powerful way to connect with your inner self. It will allow you to dive deep into your consciousness and become one with your personal spirituality. Meditation is a method that enhances your awakening process while illuminating your mental awareness. While meditating, you should always make sure your surrounding area is as neat as possible. If there is too much clutter or disorder in the area, the frequency levels will be disoriented. Once you begin your meditation, push your tongue against the ceiling of your mouth so that the vibration from humming and mantras can shock the pineal gland. I personally encourage you to create your own mantra in order to connect to your personal essence. Nothing is wrong with using a mantra that is created for a specific reason, but by using your own mantra it will connect you to the most sacred place within yourself. In conjunction with your mantra, you can also incorporate a personal ritual that becomes a sacred routine. It can be as simple as drinking a glass of water in three increments while lighting three separate candles before you meditate. This practice will be interconnected to your own spirituality, therefore, no one else can tap into it. Liberation through meditation has been a sacred method since the ancient times of our ancestors. This is why we must use this practice in our daily lives and pass it on to the future generations to come.

Part 5. Liberation through Revolutionary Tactics

When dealing with a Revolutionary stance for liberation I'll keep it short and sweet. First and foremost, I do not advocate for the use of unnecessary violence. Protecting myself and my loved ones is the only time I would resort to violence. With that being said, every melanated community needs to organize and train themselves on the structure of militant actions and reactions. We're living in a time where the KKK is still relevant; regular citizens are killing unarmed melanated men; and the cops are shooting us daily. There's no telling what the near future will bring, so preparing for the worst is imperative!

Affecting the economic structure within your country is another Revolutionary Tactic that holds value. When being mistreated socially, a good ole boycott can make a huge impact. We all remember how the bus boycotts in the mid 1950s damaged the transportation economy immensely. If we had created our own transportation companies instead of going back to theirs, we would've generated a large substantial amount of wealth for ourselves. I understand the difficulties of sustaining black owned businesses in those times, but it would have been worth a shot. It's now the year 2021 and "Melanated America" holds a great deal of power concerning the economy. We circulate nearly 2 trillion dollars annually, so imagine if we direct most of that currency to our own businesses. This would almost immediately shake up the crooked economic structure here in America. Making a Revolutionary stance can be done in ways which needs no violence. We have to gain the courage to stand up and attack our current conditions at any means necessary just as the Bro. Malcolm stated. So, if it means hurting the pockets of those who choose to carry on with social injustice; **SO BE IT!!!**

Part 6. Liberation of the Soul (A Metaphysical Concept)

The ancient Kemites (Egyptians) knew that the SOUL was a star that is trapped inside of the physical body. In "Stolen Legacy" George G. M James explains how the ancient Priest (master teacher) of the Mystery System taught a concept which states that the body is only a tomb for the soul. True salvation of the soul happens when man purely knows himself (know thyself). In order to gain knowledge of self he/she must look within and conquer every element of oneness. The very moment that man reaches a state of enlightenment his **Kundalini energy** will flow up the spine and ignite the **third eye chakra** (pineal gland) and **crown chakra** . This process will project your awareness into a higher heavenly dimension of the universe. The euphoric experience will then expand your consciousness into spiritual realms far beyond the comprehension of 3rd dimensional (3D) thought. Once this process is cyclic, your soul will become liberated and salvation will be rewarded.

Chapter III. Knowledge of Self

"Be strong in a weak world; seek knowledge in a lost world; then you can wake up in a sleeping world; understand who you are first before understanding the complexity of the world..."

-Bro. Lyle

Part 1. Know Thyself

"Man **K**now **T**hyself**"** is a phrase that comes from the ancient Kemetic (Egyptian) teachings. It is widely regarded as the most powerful phrase mentioned in the existence of humanity. Knowledge of self is by far one of the most integral aspects of self-liberation. The late Great Marcus Garvey stated that *"A people without the knowledge of their past history, origin and culture is like a tree without roots."* To go even deeper, my input to his quote is as follows: *"If the roots of a tree are artificial, how can you expect it to produce real fruit?"* We have to understand that self-knowledge must be obtained through sound and relentless research without bias. Gaining knowledge from a one-sided point of view is useless. You have to take the good with the bad in all instances.

Modern Western education is not geared to teach the melanated people their true history. Expecting to gain knowledge of self through their institutions is erroneous. These educational institutes are set up to keep the minds of the oppressed shackled. Using simple observational skills will help decipher every motive of their systematic agenda. Just think logically on how all black history starts with slavery when taught in school. The "system" never teaches the melanated child about all the **GREAT** accomplishments their ancestors gained in antiquity. We never learned about ancient Kemet (Egypt), Moorish Empire, Mali Empire, The Dogon Tribe, The Olmecs etc. All we saw in the history books were white men doing great things while the melanated man struggled to sustain any form of normality. This is how they write us out of history and devalue our contributions to society. A group of people who wish to keep another group oppressed would be crazy to tell them about their significant truth. To be honest, this ideology is the perfect weapon for controlling the minds of the masses. With these observations in plain sight, we must take the proper steps towards liberation very seriously.

A brief summary on how Ancient Kemet (Egypt) valued the "Know Thy Self" concept.

Above the entrance of most temples and lodges in Ancient Kemet (Egypt), serving as an academic scientific Learning Center, appeared the phrase "Man Know Thyself". Knowledge of self has always been the root of complete and thorough education in ancient Kemetic teachings called the mystery systems. (see -*Stolen Legacy by George GM James*) The word education comes from the Latin term, Educo/Educare meaning to draw out, to bring out, and lead out of. Thus, the true source of knowledge and education begins deep inside each person. With this understanding, the foundation of proper education is knowledge of self. We need to exercise honest personal analysis and correct weaknesses that may interfere with our purpose and aspirations.

All new students of the ancient Kemetic mystery systems we're called initiates. Before the initiates could even be permitted to enter the sacred education process they were required to purge themselves of physical, spiritual and mental toxins. This cleansing was essential for the preparation process. It included fasting, meditation and supplication to humble the inner spirit and harness the human passions. Once one gains a full understanding and acceptance of personal tendencies, motivations, positives, and negatives the journey can begin towards applying knowledge of self. This will empower us to access our inheritance gifts from the Creator and cultivate the wisdom that is gained from personal, spiritual, and academic experiences.

Ancient Kemetic Proverbs

"Know the World in Yourself. Never look for Yourself in the World for this would be to project your illusion."

"The Kingdom of Heaven is within you; and whosoever shall know himself shall find it."

"The purpose of all human life is to achieve a state of consciousness apart from bodily concerns."

"Silence is of great profit. An abundance of speech profiteth nothing. If one comes to thee full of knowledge, listen and heed, for wisdom is all. Keep thou not silent when evil is spoken for Truth like the sunlight shines above all."

"The student will read between the lines and gain wisdom. If the light is in you, the light which is engraved in these tablets will respond."

"The man who knows how to lead one of his brothers towards what he has known may one day be saved by that very brother."; "True teaching is not an accumulation of knowledge; it is an awakening of consciousness which goes through successive stages."

"The womb of the woman is the most sacred place on earth. When you believe this, when you know this, you cannot allow an UNQUALIFIED man inside."

"All things are possible. Who you are is limited by who you think you are."

<u>An African Proverb (A.) "How long have we existed?"</u>

A wise man was once asked about the timeline of human existence by one of his students. The wise man pointed to the night sky and said to the student, *"Count every star in the sky then you will know how long we have existed; count every drop of water in the oceans then you will know how long we have existed; count every grain of soil in the earth and then you will know how long we have existed."* We have existed since existence. Our souls have always been in the Universe since the beginning of The All. We the cosmos people exist according to a cyclic time frame not a linear time frame. As SOULS, we chose to come down to Earth and take on this human experience. Always remember that the body is just a tomb for the soul.

An African Proverb (B.) "The Nature And History of (The Sun People and The Ice People)"

Once upon a time there was a group of people called the **Sun People** and **The Ice People**. The Sun People lived under the gracious warmth of vibrant rays created from the mighty Sun. The Sun gave them a vast amount of essential elements needed to sustain life. There were three seasons per year of prosperous farming consisting of vegetation, fruit, and produce. These people lived in complete harmony with nature because it taught them natural principles and morals about life itself. When it came down to protecting one's goods, there was very little concern about stolen property because everything was in abundance. Trading was extremely popular amongst different tribes throughout the land; therefore, it began to stimulate economic growth. This partnership created a great deal of respect between them and laid the foundations down for civilization.

Let us now view the situations surrounding people of the ice. The Ice People had to endure a far more challenging geographical condition. Living in the northern caves of the Caucasus Mountains, there was maybe one month out the year that enabled them to grow any sort of food source. The skies were almost always dim with an overcast covering the sun. Mountains of snow would fall onto the land making it nearly impossible to maintain habitable living conditions. Having very minimal amounts of resources created a vicious "survival of the fittest" mindset, which eventually translated throughout most of their existence. During the long harsh winters, the Ice People were forced to attack other nearby tribes and salvage as many necessities possible for surviving. It's also proven that these people were forced to become cannibals due to the lack of food source. Consequently, the Ice People began to hate nature because nature never blessed them.

One day the Ice People started to migrate towards the southern hemisphere in search of better living conditions. When they finally reached the land of The Sun People, they witnessed the most amazing things their eyes have ever seen. Fruits were just falling off trees by the dozens; vegetable crops were covering large fields; gold and diamonds were plentiful; and herds of cattle were running around freely. The Sun People accepted them with open arms while teaching them their ways of life. The more and more the Sun People taught them, the more they became envious due to the previous neglections nature showed for ages. Once the Ice People learned enough skills to become self-sufficient, they began to strategize ways to conquer the Sun People and eventually steal their land. This was the nature that was instilled in the Ice People from centuries of near starvation, wars, clever deceitfulness, and horrific climates. So, with this understanding of events, we can decipher why certain things are happening in this day in time.

Part 2. You Are A STAR

As we gain wisdom pertaining to Knowledge of Self, we must also have a sound understanding of our biological makeup. The human body is composed of the same elements that are in the stars of our universe. While examining this unique fact, you will discover that our bodies contain 65% Oxygen; 18.5% Carbon; 9.5% Hydrogen; 3.3% Nitrogen and several other key elements (Calcium, Phosphorus, Potassium, Sulfur, Magnesium, Sodium, Iron,etc.). These elements are the exact ones found in stars and other cosmic phenomena. In Karel Schriver's book "Living With The Stars", he explains how we are intimately linked to the Sun's nuclear; the collisions with asteroids; and the cycle lifespan of stars. Within the core of a star, a process called nucleosynthesis occurs. Nucleosynthesis is basically the makings of elements. Once a star's life cycle is complete, all the elements that were generated inside will sweep out into the cosmic realms of the universe. Then another generation is formed from those elements and this process will continue on forever. Every element in existence was made from stars. The unique thing about it, is that once these elements are combined in different ways, you can make minerals, gases, asteroids etc. From asteroids you can start creating planets then water and other necessities needed to sustain life and then, eventually, humans.

The Principle Of Correspondence ("As above so below...As within so as without...") exemplifies the fact that everything in the universe is of one part. You are the universe, and the universe is you. There are approximately 7.9 billion universes on planet Earth, meaning that each and every person is their own sacred universe which is linked to the "ALL" consciousness.

<u>Part 3. The 7 Ancient Hermetic Principles of Prophetic Wisdom (Kush/Kemet/Egypt) aka The 7 Universal Laws</u>

The 7 Hermetic Principles are divine laws that govern the universe. These principles are intimately permeated throughout all existence, from cosmic consciousness to the very nature of humans and nature itself. Each one of these principles can interconnect with the other, therefore, we can now understand those sacred unions within the Universal ALL.

1.) **The Principle of Mentalism** - ("The ALL is MIND; The Universe is Mental") This Principle embodies the truth that "All is Mind." It explains that The **ALL** (which is the Substantial Reality underlying all the outward manifestations and appearances which we know under the terms of "The Material Universe"; the "Phenomena of Life"; "Matter"; "Energy"; and, in short, all that is apparent to our material senses) is Spirit, which in itself is unknowable and undefinable, but which may be considered and thought of as an infinite, universal, living mind. It also explains that our phenomenal world is simply a mental creation of The **ALL**, and that the universe as a whole has its existence in the **Mind** of The **ALL**, in which we "live, move, and have our being." An understanding of this great Hermetic Principle of Mentalism enables the individual to readily grasp the laws of the Mental Universe, and to apply the same to his well-being and advancement. This Principle also explains the true nature of "Energy," "Power," and "Matter," and why or how all these are subordinate to the Mastery of **Mind**. One of the old Hermetic Masters wrote, many ages ago: "He who grasps the truth of the Mental Nature of the Universe is well advanced on The Path to Mastery." And these words are as true today as at the time they were first spoken.

2.) **The Principle of Vibration** - ("Nothing rests; everything moves; everything vibrates.") This Principle embodies the truth that "everything is in motion"; "everything vibrates"; "nothing is at rest"; facts which Modern Science endorses, and which each new scientific discovery tends to verify. And yet this Hermetic Principle was articulated thousands of years ago, by the Masters of Ancient Kemet. This Principle explains that the differences between different manifestations of Matter, Energy, Mind, and Spirit, result largely from varying rates of vibration. Everything from The **ALL**, which is Pure Consciousness & Spirit, down to the grossest form of Matter is in constant vibration. The higher the vibrations are, the higher the position in the scale will be. The vibration of Spirit is at such an infinite rate of intensity and rapidity that it is practically at rest just as a rapidly moving wheel seems to be motionless. At the other end of the scale, there are gross forms of matter whose vibrations are so low that they also seem to be at rest. Between these poles, there are millions upon millions of varying degrees of vibration. From corpuscle and electron, atom and molecule, to worlds and universes, everything is in vibratory motion. This is also true on the planes of energy and force (which are but varying degrees of vibration); and also on the mental planes (whose states depend upon vibrations); and even on to the spiritual planes. An understanding of this Principle, with the appropriate formulas, enables Hermetic students to control their own mental vibrations as well as those of others. The Masters also apply this Principle to the conquering of Natural phenomena, in various ways. "He who understands the Principle of Vibration, has grasped the sceptre of power...."

3.) **The Principle of Correspondence** - ("As above, so as below; as below, so above. As within, so without; as without, so within") This Principle embodies the truth that there is always a correspondence between the laws and phenomena of the various planes of Being and Life. By understanding this Principle, you will embody the art of solving dark paradoxes, and the hidden secrets of Nature. There are planes beyond our knowledge, but when we apply the Principle of Correspondence to them, we are able to understand much that would otherwise be unknown to us.

This Principle is of universal application and manifestation on the various planes of the material and spiritual universe. In other words, everything that is of the cosmos is the same elements residing on earth. It can be revealed either as a physical or a spiritual interpretation. Correspondence is an Universal Law.   .

4.) **The Principle of Polarity** - ("Everything is Dual and has poles or opposites; opposites are identical in nature, but different in degree") This Principle embodies the truth that "everything is dual"; "everything has two poles"; "everything has its pair of opposites," all of which were old Hermetic axioms. It explains the old paradoxes, that have perplexed so many, which have been stated as follows: "Thesis and antithesis are identical in nature, but different in degree"; "opposites are the same, differing only in degree"; "the pairs of opposites may be reconciled"; "extremes meet"; "everything is and isn't, at the same time"; "all truths are but half-truths"; "every truth is half-false"; "there are two sides to everything," etc. It explains that in everything there are two poles, or opposite aspects, and that "opposites" are really only the two extremes of the same thing, with many varying degrees between them. To illustrate: Heat and Cold, although "opposites," are really the same thing, the differences consisting merely of degrees of the same thing. Look at your thermometer and see if you can discover where "heat" terminates and "cold" begins! There is no such thing as "absolute heat" or "absolute cold"—the two terms "heat" and "cold" simply indicate varying degrees of the same thing, and that "same thing" which manifests as "heat" and "cold" is merely a form, variety, and rate of Vibration. So "heat" and "cold" are simply the "two poles" of that which we call "Heat"; and the phenomena attendant thereupon are manifestations of the Principle of Polarity. The same Principle manifests in the case of "Light and Darkness," which are the same thing, the difference consisting of varying degrees between the two poles of the phenomena. Where does "darkness" leave off, and "light" begin? What is the difference between "Large and Small"? Between "Hard and Soft"? Between "Black and White"? Between "Sharp and Dull"? Between "Noise and Quiet"? Between "High and Low"? Between "Positive and Negative"? The same Principle operates on the Mental Plane. Let us take a radical and extreme example of "Love and Hate," two mental states apparently, totally different. And yet there are degrees of Hate and degrees of Love, and a middle point in which we use the terms "Like or Dislike," which shade into each other so gradually that sometimes we are at a loss to know whether we "like" or "dislike" or "neither." All are simply degrees of the same thing, as you can clearly see. It's also possible to change the vibrations of Hate to vibrations of Love in one's own mind and in the minds of others. The Principle of Polarity explains these paradoxes, and no other Principle can supersede it.

5.) **The Principle of Rhythm** - ("Everything flows, out and in; everything has its tides; all things rise and fall; the pendulum-swing") This Principle embodies the truth that in everything there is manifested motion, to and fro; a flow and inflow; a swing backward and forward; a pendulum-like movement; a high-tide and low-tide. There is always an action and a reaction; an advance and a retreat; a rising and a sinking. This is in the affairs of the Universe, sun, earth, men, animals, mind, energy, and matter. Rhythm also manifests itself in the creation and destruction of worlds; in the rise and fall of nations; in the life of all things; and finally in the mental states of Man (and it is with this latter that the Hermetists find the understanding of the Principle most important). The Hermetists have grasped this Principle, finding its universal application and have also discovered certain means to overcome its effects in themselves by the use of appropriate formulas and methods.

6.) **The Principle of Cause and Effect** - ("Every Cause has its Effect; every Effect has its Cause; everything happens according to law") This Principle embodies the fact that there is a Cause for every Effect; an Effect from every Cause. It explains that: "Everything Happens according to Law"; that nothing ever "merely happens"; that there is no such thing as Chance; that while there are various planes of Cause and Effect, the higher dominating the lower planes, still nothing ever entirely escapes the Law. The Hermetists understood the art and methods of rising above the ordinary plane of Cause and Effect. By mentally rising to a higher plane they became Causers instead of Effects.

7.) **The Principle of Gender** -("Gender is in everything; everything has its Masculine and Feminine Principles") This Principle embodies the truth that there is gender manifested in everything. The Masculine and Feminine Principles are eternal. This is true not only of the Physical Plane, but of the Mental and even the Spiritual Planes. On the Physical Plane, the Principal manifests as sex, on the higher planes it takes higher forms, but the Principle is forever the same. No creation, physical, mental or spiritual, is possible without this Principle. An understanding of its laws will throw light on many subjects that has perplexed the minds of men. The Principle of Gender works ever in the direction of generation, regeneration, and creation. Everything, and every person, contains the two Elements or Principles, or this great Principle, within it, him or her. Every Male thing has the Female Element also; every Female contains also the Male Principle. If you would understand the philosophy of Mental and Spiritual Creation, Generation, and Re-generation, you must understand and study this Hermetic Principle. It contains the solution of many mysteries of Life. *(Some extracted information from "The Kybalion" by The Tree Initiates)*

Part 4. Great Empires of Ancient Alkebulan (Africa/Afrikka)

Ancient Alkebulan (Africa) was and still is the center of all. Every great Empire emerged from all parts of the illustrious motherland. Melanated people ruled throughout the continent and eventually migrated and gave the rest of the world LIFE. Civilization as we know it was created inside of her. Before we begin on the topic of great empires there's one thing we must clear up for the sake of understanding. The original name of Africa was considered to be Alkebulan which means mother of mankind or Garden of Eden. Alkebulan is the oldest word of indigenous origin (according to some scholars). Moving forward, we should also know that Africa was also divided by European colonizers during the Berlin Conference 1884-1885. When we see modern maps of Africa today, it is a depiction of how colonizers drew up borders and split areas up for themselves. So, when I mention these great nations of people and empires, please understand that most original names have been changed by the Europeans.

History reveals to us the many great ancient empires of Africa. Realizing the significance of it's great achievement is extremely important for the melanated people to be aware of. Being put down as not contributing much to society is still embedded in the minds of a lot of our people. George G.M James explains in his book *"Stolen Legacy"* how ancient Egyptians first introduced the educational curriculum as we know it today. They taught about the Seven Liberal Arts, secret systems of languages, mathematical symbolism and magic. Political and philosophical traditions also come from the ancient Egyptians teachings. In Cheikh Anta Diop's book *("The African Origin of Civilization Myth or Reality")* he explains how Plato and Aristotle use their teachings from ancient Kemet (Egypt) to form their political ideas which is the earliest structure of European politics. By knowing these few facts there has to be a level of pride when remembering our ancestors.

In my adolescent years I never was taught about the first civilizations of Kush (Ethiopia), Kemet (Egypt), Mali, the Kongos, the Americas, Australia and Asia. Melanated people were the original rulers of the Earth. We were kings, queens, doctors, scientists, teachers, philosophers, architects, lawyers and warriors. Uncovering these facts may unsettle some, but everything that's said is historically documented. Once again, I urge my fellow brethren to embrace your ancestral achievements and take them to new heights for generational empowerment.

A Brief Summary Of Ancient Kingdoms In Alkebulan (Africa)

The following African civilizations, warriors, and inventions that I will be briefly summarizing are just portions of the greatness we contributed to society. I'm not attempting to dive into great detail about each Empire, because that itself would be an entirely different book. My purpose is only to shed light on some of our forgotten history. With that in mind, view these summaries as sample size footnotes for further research.

Kush (Ethiopia)

The Kingdom of Kush was an ancient African kingdom situated on the junction of the Blue Nile, White Nile and River Atbara in what is now the Republic of Sudan. The first Kingdom of Kush, also known as Kerma, is one of if not the oldest African states. Kerma arose around 2400 B.C., and had become the capital of the Kush Kingdom by 2000 B.C. Kush reached its zenith between 1750 and 1500 B.C. -a time known as Classical Kerma. Kush flourished most when Egypt was at its weakest, and the last 150 years of the Classical Kerma period overlap with a time of upheaval in Egypt known as the Second Intermediate Period (1650 to 1500 B.C.). During this era, Kush had access to gold mines and traded extensively with its northern neighbors while generating significant wealth and power.

The second Kush kingdom was established after the Bronze Age collapse and the disintegration of the New Kingdom of Kemet (Egypt). It was centered at Napata in its early phase. After King Kashta ("the Kushite") invaded Egypt in the 8th century BC, the Kushite kings ruled as pharaohs of the Twenty-fifth dynasty of Egypt for a century, until they were expelled by Psamtik I in 656 BC.

The power of the 25th Dynasty (the second Kingdom of Kush) reached a climax under the pharaohs Piye and Taharqa. The Nile valley empire was as large as it had been since the New Kingdom. The 25th dynasty ushered in a renaissance period for Ancient Egypt. Religion, the arts, and architecture were restored to their glorious Old, Middle, and New Kingdom forms. Pharaohs, such as Taharqa, built or restored temples and monuments throughout the Nile valley, including at Memphis, Karnak, Kawa, Jebel Barkal, etc. It was during the 25th dynasty that the Nile valley saw the first widespread construction of pyramids (many in modern Sudan) since the Middle Kingdom. Taharqa was the son of Piye and the first seventeen years of his reign were very prosperous for Kush.

(The temple of Amun at Naqa, Kush, photo credit Adrew Crowe)

(Meroe is an ancient city on the east bank of the Nile; Kush (Ethiopia)...)

Kemet (Egypt)

Ancient Kemet (Egypt) was one of the greatest and most powerful empires in the history of the world. It lasted for over three thousand years from 3150 BC to 30 B.C. as described by modern scholars. Some earlier scholars such as Chekh Anta Diop argue that the empire in fact lasted for nearly 17,000 years or more. The civilization of ancient Kemet (Egypt) was located along the Nile River in northwest Africa. The Nile was the source of much of Egypt's wealth. The Egyptians became experts in irrigation and were able to use water from the Nile to grow rich and profitable crops. Their inventions and technology had an impact on many civilizations that were created after its glory days. They were able to construct large pyramids, temples, and lodges with ramps, lever mechanisms and sacred metaphysics **(secret levitation liquid and powder, which is disclosed to the masses)**. Language and writing systems were also two of the most important inventions of that time. Those systems were called "Medu Neter" (hieroglyphics). The writing allowed Egyptians to keep accurate records of historical accounts, ancient teachings, and ritual practices. Those writings also helped to maintain control of the empire through political ideologies. Other inventions included papyrus sheets, medicine remedies, mathematics and geometry for building, business transactions, toothpaste, political philosophies, educational institutions, astronomy and much more.

(Kemetic Judgement scene/ The weighing of the Heart; where the modern Judicial system comes from)

(Ancient Sculptures from Kush and Kemet Dynastic Periods; Defaced to hide true identity)

(The Great Temple at Abu Simbel; Ramesses II)

The Mali Empire

The founding of the Mali Empire dates to the 1200s c.e, when a ruler named Sundiata Keita sometimes called "Lion King" led a revolt against a Sasso King and united his subjects into a new state. Under Keita and his successors, the empire tightened its grips over a large part of West Africa and grew rich in trade. Its most important cities were Djenne' and Timbuktu, both of which were renowned for their elaborate adobe mosques and Islamic schools. One such institution, Timbuktu's Sankore University which included a library with estimated 700,000 manuscripts. The Mali Empire eventually disintegrated in the 16th century, but at its peak it was one of the jewels of the African continent and was known over the world for its wealth and luxury. One legendary tale about the Kingdom's richest concerns the ruler Mansa Musa, who made a stop over in Egypt during the 14th century pilgrimage to Mecca. According to contemporary sources, Mensa passed out so much gold during the visit that he caused its value to plummet in Egyptian markets for several years. No one actually knows exactly how much riches the Empire possessed but it is said to be one of the wealthiest of all times.

(The Grand Mosque of Djenne; Mali Empire; photo credit GlobalGaz)

Moors in Spain

In the year 711 A.D the Moorish army under the leadership of Tariq ibn-Ziyad crossed the strait of Gibraltar from northern Africa and invaded the Iberian Peninsula "Andalus". After conquering Spain, the Moors ruled for over 800 years. They introduced new scientific teachings to Europe such as an astrolabe, a device for measuring the position of the stars and planets. They also bought scientific progress in astronomy, chemistry, physics, mathematics, geography and philosophy. At its zenith, Cordova, the heart of Moorish territory in Spain was the most modern city in Europe. They brought powered streets to the land and during the nights 10 miles of streets were well illuminated by lamps. This was hundreds of years before Paris and London had paved streets and Street lamps. They also brought public baths and proper sanitation to the region. The Moors introduced new crops such as the orange, lemon, peach apricot, fig, sugarcane, ginger, cotton, and silk which remain some of Spain's main products today. There are so many other contributions that were made including early libraries to the early medical instruments. Sadly the empire was taken down and 1492 by the same people they helped to advance. The Legacy of The Moors in Spain will forever be appreciated.

The Olmecs (Xi) In the Americas

The Olmecs were the first major civilizations in Mexico. They lived in the tropical lowlands on the Gulf of Mexico and in present day Mexican states of Veracruz and Tabasco. The Olmec name is a Nahuatl Aztec language word which means the rubber people. They are the first people to figure out how to convert the latex of the rubber tree into something that could be shaped, cured and hardened. Olmecs were among the first Mesoamerican complex societies around 1600 B.C.E and their culture influenced many later civilizations such as the Maya Civilization. They are known for the immense stone heads they carved from volcanic rock called basalt. Their artifacts have been found across Mesoamerica indicating that there were extensive interregional trade routes. Trading helped them build urban centers of San Corenza and Laventa. This great ancient civilization is further proof that Africans were settled in the Americas ages before the Trans-Atlantic Slave Trade.

(Ancient negroid stone heads in the Olmec heartland 1600 B.C; photo credit Steven Bridger)

The Dogon Tribe

The Dogon is a tribe that resides in Mali, West Africa. They are believed to be the descendants of the ancient Egyptians and their astronomical genius goes back thousands of years to around 3200 BC. According to their traditions, the star Sirius has a companion star which is invisible to the human eye. This companion star has a 50-year elliptical orbit around the visible Sirius and is extremely heavy. The invisible star also rotates on its axis. How did people who lacked any kind of astronomical devices know so much about an invisible star? The star Sirius B was not photographed until it was done by a large telescope in 1970. The Dogon also told stories of the planet Jupiter stating that it possesses four major moons. They also knew of Saturn's rings and that the planets orbit the sun. These stories were all facts told in tradition thousands of years ago but were discovered by Westerners only after Galileo invented the telescope.

The Songhai Empire

The Songhai Empire was undoubtedly one of the largest Empires to ever exist. Formed in the 15th century from some of the former regions of the Mali Empire, this West African kingdom was larger than western Europe and comprised parts of a dozen modern day nations. The empire enjoyed a period of prosperity thanks to vigorous trade policies and a sophisticated bureaucratic system that separated its vast holdings into different provinces, each ruled by its own governor. It reached its zenith in the early 16th century under the rule of the devout King Muhammad I Askia, who conquered new lands forged in alliance with Egypt's Muslim Caliph and established hundreds of Islamic schools in Timbuktu. While the Songhai Empire was once among the most powerful states in the world, it later crumbled in the late 1500s after a period of civil war and internal strife left it open to an invasion by the Sultan of Morocco.

(The Tomb of Askia, emperor of the Songhai Empire)

The Great Zimbabwe

The Zimbabwe kingdom ruled over a large area of modern-day Botswana, Zimbabwe and Mozambique. It was particularly rich in cattle and precious metals. There were several trade routes that connected the region's gold fields with ports on the Indian Ocean cost. Though little is known about its history the remains of artifacts such as Chinese pottery, Arabian glass and Egyptian textiles indicate that it was once a well connected mercantile center. One of the most impressive monuments in Sub-Saharan Africa is The Great Zimbabwe, an imposing collection of stacked boulders, stone towers, and defensive walls assembled from cut granite blocks. The rock citadel has long been the subject of myths and legends. It was once thought to be the residence of the Biblical Queen Sheba but historians now know it as the capital city of an indigenous empire that thrived in the region between the 13th and 15th centuries. The fortress city of Great Zimbabwe was mysteriously abandoned sometime in the 15th century after the kingdom went into decline.

(Ancient Architecture of the Great Zimbabwe)

<u>The Benin Empire</u>

The Benin Empire was founded in what is now modern day Nigeria and was considered one of the oldest most developed states in West Africa until its annexation by the British Empire. They were famous for artisans crafted masterpieces from ivory, bronze and iron. The Benin Empire had a strong trading relationship with the Portuguese, exchanging palm oil, pepper, and ivory for currency and firearms. The relationship even saw an ambassador visit Lisbon in the 16th century. Britain's first expedition to Benin occurred in 1553 and a mutually beneficial trading relationship existed throughout the 16th & 17th centuries. The relationship ended when Benin suspected Britain of making controlling advancements that would threaten Benin's power.

(Mid 16-17th century copper alloy plaque Benin art)

(18 century bronze art Head of an Oba)

Part 5. Great Warriors

Shaka Zulu (1787 C.E - 1828 C.E)

In my personal opinion, Shaka Zulu was the greatest warrior who ever walked the face of this earth. He was born into the small South African clan of the Zulus in 1787. His father was the chief of the Zulus and his mother Nandi was the daughter of the chief who ruled a nearby clan. When Shaka was young his father drove him and his mother out of the village. They were disgraced and forced to find refuge with another clan. He and his mother became part of Chief Dingiswayo's powerful clan known as the Mthethwa in 1802. Shaka began his training as a warrior and quickly discovered ways to improve the method of fighting. During his training he began to walk around barefoot in order to toughen up his feet which ignited a more mental strengthening. Shaka felt like this would enable him to become more agile in battle and help him to maneuver better in close quarters. His strength, courage, and unique fighting methods made him the most furious warrior in the land.

When Shaka's father died, he became chief of the Zulu, and when Dingiswayo died he took control over both tribes while becoming the most powerful leader in the region. At the peak of Shaka's reign he was in charge of 50,000 combatants and reigned over 250,000 people. Even though he had the power to defeat many, war was not his first decision. He was a skillful diplomat who incorporated other techniques to negotiate with the enemy. Tragically, Shaka's legacy was cut short by the betrayal of his own brothers who assassinated him at the age of 41.

(Shaka Zulu statue site in Stanger in the Kwa Zulu-Natak province of South Africa)

<u>Mansa Musa (1280 C.E - 1337 C.E)</u>

Mansa Musa has been described as the wealthiest person in history. At the time of his ascension to the throne, Mali pretty much consisted of the territory of the former Ghana Empire which Mali had conquered. Mansa was credited for conquering over 24 cities. At that time Mali was perhaps the largest producer of gold in the entire world. This is why Mansa has been viewed as one of the richest people to ever walk the face of the earth. His pilgrimage to Mecca made him well known across northern Africa and the Middle East. Between the years 1324 and 1325 is when he made his legendary pilgrimage. It was said that 60,000 men wore brocade and Persian silk clothing on the journey. There were also 12,000 slaves who each carried 11.8kg of gold bars who accompanied him on the voyage. Because of Mansa's generosity of donating large amounts of gold he created a ten-year gold recession in the cities of Cairo, Medina and Mecca.

(Mansa Musa of the Mali Empire)

Hannible (c. 247 BCE - 183 BCE)

Contrary to popular belief, Hannibal was not of European descent. Historical evidence shows that Hannibal's ethnicity was Phoenician which was earlier called Canaanites. He was born into a Carthaginian military family and made to swear hostility towards Rome.

During the Second Punic War, Hannibal swept across southern Europe and through the Alps constantly defeating the Roman army, but never taking the city itself. The army consisted of over 100,000 troops and nearly 40 huge war elephants. For most of the time Hannibal fought with little support from Carthage. He was able to inflict heavy casualties on the Roman army in the battles of Trebbia, Trasimene and Cannae, but at a major expense to his men and war elephants.

Meanwhile, Rome dispatched forces to Iberia and North Africa, raiding Carthaginian towns and villages. In 203 B.C Hannibal abandoned his Roman campaign and traveled back to defend his country. In 202 BC the two armies met at the Battle of Zama, where unlike in the previous meeting, the Romans had superior forces. They used trumpets to confuse the elephants by making them circle back and trampled many of the Carthaginian troops. Hannibal's army was scattered and many of the soldiers were hunted and killed by the Romans.

The Roman peace treaties were extremely harsh on the Carthaginians, severely reducing their military and extracting large reparations. After being elected a chief magistrate, Hannibal spent the next several years in Carthaginian politics. At this time, he instituted elections for military judges and changed terms of office from life to two years.

Gen. Jean-Jacques Dessalines (1804 Haitian Revolution)

The Haitian Revolution has often been described as the largest and most successful slave rebellion in the Western Hemisphere. Slaves initiated the rebellion in 1791 and by 1804 they had succeeded in ending not just slavery but French control over the colony. The Haitian Revolution, however, was much more complex, consisting of several revolutions going on simultaneously. These revolutions were influenced by the French Revolution of 1789, which would come to represent a new concept of human rights, universal citizenship, and participation in government.

In the 18th century, Saint Domingue, as Haiti was then known, became France's wealthiest overseas colony, largely because of its production of sugar, coffee, indigo, and cotton generated by an enslaved labor force. When the French Revolution broke out in 1789 there were five distinct sets of interest groups in the colony. There were white planters—who owned the plantations and the slaves—and *petit blancs*, who were artisans, shopkeepers and teachers. Some of them also owned a few slaves. Together they numbered 40,000 of the colony's residents. Many of the whites in Saint Domingue began to support an independence movement that began when France imposes steep tariffs on the items imported into the colony. The planters were extremely disenchanted with France because they were forbidden to trade with any other nation. Furthermore, the white population of Saint-Dominique did not have any representation in France; they had retreated deep into the mountains of Saint Domingue and lived off subsistence. Despite their calls for independence, both the planters and *petit blancs* remained committed to the institution of slavery.

The three remaining groups were of African descent: those who were free, those who were slaves, and those who had run away. There were about 30,000 free black people in 1789. Half of them were mulatto and often they were wealthier than the *petit blancs*. The slave population was close to 500,000. Haiti had a history of slave rebellions; the slaves were never willing to submit to their status and with their strength in numbers (10 to 1) colonial officials and planters did all that was possible to control them. Despite the harshness and cruelty of Saint Dominigue slavery, there were slave rebellions before 1791. One plot involved the poisoning of masters.

Inspired by events in France, a number of Haitian-born revolutionary movements emerged simultaneously. They used as their inspiration the French Revolution's "Declaration of the Rights of Man." The General Assembly in Paris responded by enacting legislation which gave the various colonies some autonomy at the local level. The legislation, which called for "all local proprietors…to be active citizens," was both ambiguous and radical. It was interpreted in Saint Domingue as applying only to the planter class and thus excluded *petit blancs* from government. Yet it allowed free citizens of color who were substantial property owners to participate. This legislation, promulgated in Paris to keep Saint Domingue in the colonial empire, instead generated a three-sided civil war between the planters, free blacks and the *petit blancs*. However, all three groups would be challenged by the enslaved black majority which was also influenced and inspired by events in France.

Led by former slave, Toussaint L' Overture, the enslaved would act first, rebelling against the planters on August 21, 1791. By 1792 they controlled a third of the island. Despite reinforcements from France, the area of the colony held by the rebels grew as did the violence on both sides. Before the fighting ended 100,000 of the 500,000 blacks and 24,000 of the 40,000 whites were killed. Nonetheless the former slaves managed to stave off both the French forces and the British who arrived in 1793 to conquer the colony, and who withdrew in 1798 after a series of defeats by l'Overture's forces. By 1801 l'Overture expanded the revolution beyond Haiti, conquering the neighboring Spanish colony of Santo Domingo (present-day Dominican Republic). He abolished slavery in the Spanish-speaking colony and declared himself Governor-General for life over the entire island of Hispaniola.

At that moment the Haitian Revolution had outlasted the French Revolution which had been its inspiration. Napoleon Bonaparte, now the ruler of France, dispatched General Charles Leclerc, his brother-in-law, and 43,000 French troops to capture L'Overture and restore both French rule and slavery. L'Overture was taken and sent to France where he died in prison in 1803. **Jean Jacques Dessalines**, one of l'Overture's generals and himself a former slave, led the revolutionaries at the Battle of Vertieres on November 18, 1803 where the French forces were defeated. On January 1, 1804, Dessalines declared the nation independent and renamed it Haiti. France became the first nation to recognize its independence. Haiti thus emerged as the first Black republic in the world, and the second nation in the western hemisphere (after the United States) to win its independence from a European power.

(Statue of Gen. Jean Jacques Dessalines)

Yaa Asantewaa

Yaa Asantewaa was a great warrior Queen who ruled over the Ashanti Kingdom in Ghana. She is remembered for her role in leading the army that fought against the British invasion.

Ezana of Axum

Ezana reigned over the Axum Kingdom during the 4th Century AD. The Axum Kingdom covered a vast region, including modern day Northern Ethiopia, Northern Somalia, Yemen, Djibouti, parts of Southern Saudi Arabia, and Eritrea.

Behanzin Hossu Bowelle

Behanzin Hossu was one of the most influential West African Kings who ruled around the latter part of the 19th century. Among his many wins was outpowering the 1890 French voyage and demanding they pay to utilize the port of Cotonou. He was a very wise and courageous king who also commanded more than 150,000 male soldiers as well as 5000 infamous Amazon women.

Cetshwayo Kampande

Cetshwayo was considered to be a real-life African hero for defeating the British. When the British invaded Zululand Cetshwayo did not shy away from the challenge instead, he sent 20,000 plus Zulu warriors to battle. At this historic battle he managed to kill Prince Napoleon who was the heir of the French throne.

Yasuke

Yasuke was a former slave who arrived in Kyoto, Japan in the 16th century A.D. When he arrived in Kyoto the people were so amazed at how tall he was, and the dark pigmentation of his skin. They climbed all over each other just to get a glimpse of the phenomenon. At this time Oda Nobunaga ruled over the samurai. Shortly after Yasuke arrived in Japan he and Nobunaga engaged in multiple intellectual conversations, therefore creating a unique bond with each other. Soon after, Yasuke began training with the samurai and moved his way up the ranks. There isn't much record on Yasuke's battle history, but he was without a doubt historically the first Black Samurai.

(Images of Yasuke and his teacher Oda Nobunaga the

leader of the Samurai)

Part 6. Great Inventions in Ancient and Modern Times

Philosophy

The average novice to history will tell you that the founding fathers of philosophy were Socrates, Plato and Aristotle who are all European Greeks. What we are not taught in the western education system is that Greek Philosophers learned their teachings from the Egyptian Priest. The learning systems of Kemet (Egypt) were called the Mystery Systems and the students were named initiates. Students from around the world would travel from great distances to attend the schools and attain as much ancient sacred knowledge as possible. Kemet (Egypt) was the center of ancient wisdom, knowledge, spiritual rituals, philosophical and scientific knowledge that spread to other regions through student initiates. Such teachings remained as oral teaching until the conquest of Egypt by Alexander the Greek (not Great) and the movement of Aristotle and his school to compile Kemetic (Egyptian) teachings, therefore claiming it as Greek philosophy. (Allen Shabazz "Black History in A Nutshell") (George G.M James "Stolen Legacy")

<u>Mathematics</u>

Most of the mathematical concepts that are used in today's curriculum was developed in prehistoric Africa long before any other civilization. Prehistoric artifacts discovered in Africa, dated 20,000 years or more suggest early attempts to quantify time by using a counting system. There was an Ishango bone found near the Semliki River which forms part of the Nile river's headwaters. The bone is considered to be over 20,000 years old and consisted of a series of marks carved in three columns running the length of the bone. De Heinzelin, its discoverer, argued that the Ishango bone shows either a tally of the earliest known demonstration of sequences or six-month lunar calendar. This finding also suggests that women were using lunar calculations to track their menstrual cycle which would place them as mathematical pioneers.

Ancient Kemites also wrote textbooks about multiplication and division of fractions and geometric formulas to calculate the area and volume of shapes over 35,000 years ago. They calculated distance, angles, and algebraic equations that were used for various tasks. Kemites also figured out that a circle has 360 degrees and was broken up into three sections of 120 degrees.

Medicine

Modern medicine and medical treatment we use today was used centuries ago in Africa. The earliest known surgery was performed in Kemet (Egypt) around 2750 B.C. Ancient Africans performed various procedures such as vaccinations, autopsies, broken bone resetting, skin grafting, dental work, caesarean sections and anesthesia long before any other civilizations. They also used extractions from plants such as salicylic acid for pain, kaolin for diarrhea and other extracts that were used to kill Gram positive bacteria. Plants that had anti-cancer properties were also discovered and used by the ancient Africans in those times. These treatments preceded all European western medical treatments in historical accounts.

Seven Liberal Arts

The seven liberal arts were first introduced in the ancient Mystery System schools of early Egypt. The liberal arts were: 1.) Grammer, 2.) Rhetoric, 3.) Logic, 4.) Geometry, 5.) Arithmetic, 6.) Astronomy, and 7.) Music (Harmony). [James "Stolen Legacy"]

Mining of Minerals

The "Lion Cave" in Swaziland located in southeast Africa, is the earliest known mine on archaeological record. The radiocarbon dating shows the mine to be about 43,000 years old.

Astronomy

Astronomy was first recorded around 10,000 B.C.E. predynastic period in Ancient Kemet (Egypt). We know this because the Sphinx (Heru-em-Akhet) was perfectly aligned with the constellation of Leo The Lion 10,000 b.c. or even earlier. By the third millennium B.C.E the Kemetic calendar system was already in place. By charting the movements of the sun and constellations, they were able to divide the year into 12 sections and developed a yearlong calendar system. The Dogon people of Mali accumulated a wealth of detailed astronomical observations of the cosmos. Most of their findings were so advanced that plenty of scholars rather give space aliens the credit instead of the great Dogon people. Centuries ago, they plotted orbits in the system extremely accurate all the way through the 20th century. The Dogon also knew about Saturn's rings, the spiral structure of the Milky Way, Jupiter's moons, and the Sirius star's orbit.

In other studies, it has been said that perhaps the Aboriginal People of Australia may have been the first astronomers. Research has revealed that aborigines were integrating oral accounts of astronomical accounts for over 50,000 years. This information makes the claim of originality even more intriguing, therefore, suggesting an even deeper investigation.

Architecture and Engineering

Many ancient African civilizations built various sophisticated environments. We all know about the great engineering feats of the Egyptians who built more than 80 pyramids. The largest of the pyramids covers 13 acres and is made of 2.25 million blocks of stone. Later on in the 12th century there were hundreds of cities in Zimbabwe and Mozambique. They built massive stone complexes which were used for housing as well as temples. The Mali empire engineered impressive cities in the 13th century also. One of its most prized cities was Timbuktu. Timbuktu boasts a vast amount of grand palaces, mosques and universities which were amongst the first our world had ever seen on such a grand scale.

Navigation

In antiquity, ancient Africans sailed to the South Americas and Asia at least hundreds of years before the Europeans. Across the land of Africa were trade routes that stretched for thousands of miles. Many ancient societies built a variety of different boats including small reed-based vessels, sailboats, and grander structures with many cabins. The Mali and Songhai also built boats 100 feet long and 20 feet in width that could carry up to 80 tons. Different genetic evidence from plants and descriptions of art from societies inhabiting South America at the time, also suggest that small numbers of West Africans sailed to the east coast of South America, and still remain there to this day.

Papyrus

Papyrus was the first prototype of the modern paper that we use today. It dates as far back as the fourth millennium B.C.E. in ancient Kemet.

Universities

The very first known university in the history of the world is The Temple of Waset (City of the Sceptre). The Temple of Waset is located in the modern Egyptian city of Luxor along the Nile. Waset was built during the reign of Amenhotep III in the XVIII Dynasty, 1405-1370 B.C.E. This university was named the "Egyptian Mystery System" by the Greeks because its teachings were foreign to them.

Education was a holistic concept in its nature. The process of education was not primarily seen as a process of acquiring knowledge. It was seen as a process of the transformation of the initiate (student) to progress through successive stages of rebirth to become more Godlike. Disciplined study under the guidance of a Priest (master teacher) was the single path to becoming a new person. The education term was 40 years with an enormous curriculum. The university had a large library with tens of thousands of scribes and manuscripts. It was divided into 5 major departments such as astronomy and astrology, geography, geology, philosophy and theology, law and communication. In "Stolen Legacy", George G. M. James states; *"Grammar, Rhetoric, and Logic were disciplines of moral nature by means of which the irrational tendencies of a human being were purged away, and he was trained to become a living witness of the Divine Logos." -George G. M. James*

Geometry and Arithmetic were sciences of transcendental space and numeration. They were the comprehension of which provided the key not only to the problems of one's being; but also to those physical ones, which are so baffling today, owing to our use of the inductive methods. Astronomy dealt with knowledge and expressions of the cosmos, which directly correlated with man and existence. Music (or Harmony) was the living practice of philosophy, which is the adjustment of human life into harmony with God. Such was the Egyptian theory of salvation, through which the individual was trained to become godlike while on earth, and in turn would move on to the next dimension after death. This was accomplished through the efforts of the individual, through the cultivation of the Arts and Sciences on one hand, and a life of virtue on the other.

<u>Martial Arts</u>

During the Middle Kingdom of ancient Kemet (Egypt), there was a burial site constructed called Beni Hasan. This cemetery is located approximately 12 miles south of modern-day Minya, which is between the regions of Asyut and Memphis. Within the cemetery there's a tomb labeled Tomb # 15. This tomb is the tomb of Baqet III who was a Great Chief during the 11th Dynasty in the 21 century B.C.E. On the eastern wall inside of Baqet's tomb, there are impressive paintings and carvings of Nubians illustrating wrestling, grappling, and various combat throwing techniques. These paintings predate any Asian or European form of martial arts by at least 1,600 plus years.

(Painting of ancient Kemetic wrestling, grappling, and combat throwing techniques at the tomb of Baqet III)

Modern Inventors

Benjamin Banneker's family was introduced to a man named Joself Levi, sometime in the 1750s. This man was carrying a unique watch with him that caught the attention of Benjamin. Young Benjamin was extremely fascinated with the watch. He then asked to borrow it from Mr. Levi and started to explore its functions immediately. Once he figured out how it worked, he wanted to build something similar, but bigger. Realizing he lacked sufficient knowledge, Benjamin turned to where he found solutions for many of his problems – books. He borrowed some books on geometry to learn about shapes; and borrowed Sir Isaac Newton's Principia to better understand the laws of motion. Armed with these, he set about building a clock made out of hand-carved wood. It took him around two years, but he finally finished building America's first clock in 1753, at the age of 22. The clock was crafted entirely out of wood. After completion, the clock continued to work accurately for over three decades.

Between the years of 1792 and 1797, Benjamin developed six annual Farmers' Almanacs and Ephemeris for Pennsylvania, Delaware, Maryland, and Virginia. This was to predict weather, tides, eclipses and seasonal changes and tips on planting crops and home medical remedies. All the information listed in these were manually calculated and compiled by him.

Lewis Latimer - Electric Lamp Bulb 1882

Paul L. Downing - Mailbox 1891

Alexander Miles - Elevator 1867

Thomas Marshall - Fire Extinguisher 1872

Garrett Morgan - Traffic Light

Charles Drew - Blood Plasma Bag 1945

Thomas A. Carrington - Stethoscope 1876

George W. Carver- Developed over 300 food, industrial, and commercial products from peanuts.

Patricia E. Bath - Laserphaco probe which made laser surgery possible 1986

Elijah McCoy- Automatic lubricator for steam engines of locomotives and ships. He also created over 50 inventions

Marie Van Brittan Brown - Created the home security system in 1966

Benjamin Banneker - Almanac 1791

George T. Sampson - Clothes Dryer 1971

Osbourn Dorsey- Door knob and Door stop 1878

Walter B. Purvis - Fountain Pen 1890

Garrett Morgan - Gas Mask 1914

George T. Grant - Golf Tee 1899

Robert F. Fleming Jr. - Guitar 1886

Walter B. Purvis - Hand Stamp 1883

Michael C. Harvey - Lantern 1884

Edmond Berger - Spark Plug 1839

Granville T. Woods - Phone Transmitter 1884

And much more!!!

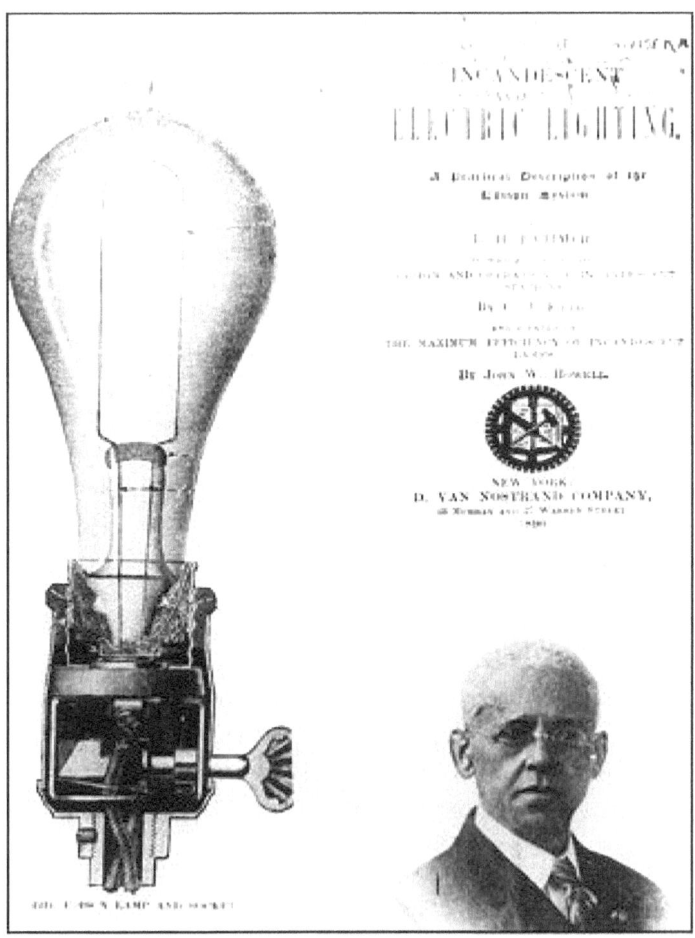

(Lewis Latimer's light bulb invention; photo credit)

https://blackinventor.com/lewis-latimer/

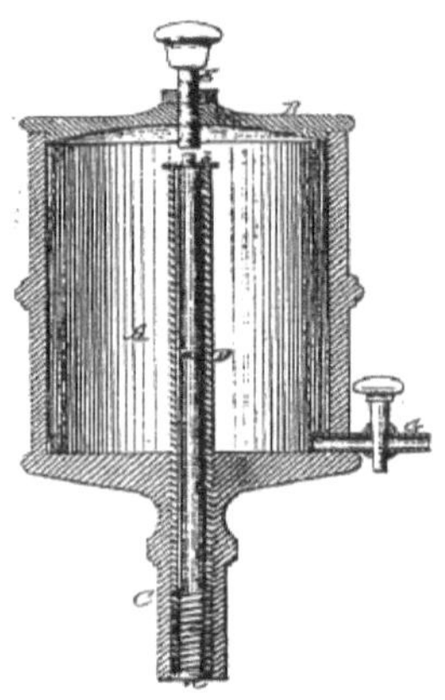

(Elijah Mccoy's Automatic Lubricator patent; The Real Mccoy photo credit)

https://aaregistry.org/story/lubricator-cup-patented/

Chapter IV. Cultural Imperialism

<u>Part 1. Cultural Imperialism explained</u>

Melanated people around the globe have been victimized by Cultural Imperialism ever since Alexander the Greek (not Great) invaded the land of Kemet (Egypt) in the year 332 B.C. We have been constantly stripped of our culture, history, spirituality, and land. Within the diaspora, most of us have no idea where our true lineage comes from. Other ethnic groups know exactly where their ancestors came from. You can ask an Asian person where he comes from and he'll tell you I'm Chinese, Japanese, Korean etc. The Caucasian man can tell you he's Irish, German, Russian, French, Italian etc. Do you see where I'm going with this? If you ask the Melanated man in America where his ancestors come from, he would have a hard time trying to answer the question. Some would simply say they're from the Motherland without knowing any specific geographic location. Others would say they are indigenous to the Americas and have **NO** ancestral connections to Africa at all. In Ivan Van Sertima's book, "They Came Before Columbus", he wrote about the discoveries of large negroid stone heads that stood 8' tall with a circumference of about 20' around. These stone heads were found in various areas of the Americas dating back as far as the 25th Dynasty of Egypt. The scholarly work of

Ivan Van Sertima has yet to be contested, this is why I do agree with us being indigenous to the Americas. The problem comes when a melanated person denies all relation to Alkebulan (Africa), and disowns their extended heritage which predates the Americas. It's really tragic how my people are so confused and misled about their ancestral lineage. You have **ONE** group of people with several totally different ideas of their origins, and it only shows yet another form of division amongst us. A major factor with this problem has to do with an obvious **"mental sedation"** from Cultural Imperialism.

On a positive note, the one thing that has not been misplaced is the soul of our people. Embedded spirituality and soul is what kept us afloat for centuries. I personally believe there's no other group of people on the planet who would have survived the atrocities that we have endured for such a long period of time. I'm not implying that no other race of people have been oppressed, but it's evident that melanated people possess a higher level of endurance.

Cultural brainwashing from (CI)

Here I will break down a few key factors that contribute to Cultural Imperialism brainwashing. Reality can be problematic to any individual who decides not to open up their minds and ignore what's right in front of them. This is why I feel compelled to unearth the hidden agendas behind our deculturalization. It's very pivotal that we understand the many tricks and schemes that are in place to mentally enslave our minds.

<u>A.) Religion</u>

Religion is the most powerful tool used by those who wish to colonize the land and minds of others. When an invader deculturizes he must first control the spiritual nature of the people whether it's voluntarily or forcefully. Knowing how sensitive this topic is, I'll begin by stating that I have no quarrels with people who are religious. The goal is to only break down the ramifications of (CI).

The etymology of the word religion means to bind or to be bound to something. Oppositely speaking, spirituality means to have self-inspiration, breath of God, breath of life, courage and pride (Latin etymology spiritus). While both may seem similar to the naked eye they are actually different in their origins etymology speaking. Religion speaks of being dependent on something, while spirituality concerns more with the individual itself. This is why I consider myself to be a spiritual person instead of religious because the Creator (The Universal ALL) is within me.

When examining religion, one must realize that it's the cultural psychological vehicle of spiritual intellectual captivity. Religion is often based on a culture. Wherever you are geographically will most likely determine your belief system. In other words, if you are from India you're Hindu; Iraq you're Muslim; Asia you're Buddhist; and Europe you're most likely Christian etc. Once again, I'm not trying to slander any belief system, but presenting a logical assessment of religion is the main objective.

A passage on ancient spirituality from "Spirituality Before Religions"(chpt. 2) by Prof. Kaba Hiawatha Kamene

Early humans in Africa saw a pattern in earthly and cosmic nature, "As above, so below." Nature taught humanity that as their consciousness grew, they would find their answers on the living Earth. While looking up into the heavens, they saw similar relationships between the living earth and the eternal heavens.

Agriculture was the key to the development of early African Spiritual philosophy. Just as the seeds of plants in the earth went through a process of conception, birth, growth, aging, death, decay, and resurrection; these early observers realized that this cycle also occurred in the animal and human world; and so too in the stars above. It was during the Neolithic period in Africa (between 18,300- 17,000) that Nature taught humans about spirituality. The development of agricultural science acted as the bridge between superstitious and belief, belief and faith, and faith and scientific knowledge of the Divine. The hidden and revealed forces of the nature of agriculture became the basis for Humanity's wisdom of the cycle of spiritual growth and ascension. African agriculturalists noticed that the planting of a man's sperm-seed within a woman's body, fertilizing her egg was like planting a seed in the earth (conception). Upon fertilization, they recorded a period of development in the earth (gestation) until the plant bloomed (human birth). The plant matured (human growth), aged, died and grew again the next season (resurrection). The sun's physical orb was not given direct credit for this creation; it was the light, heat, and sound energy emitted from the sun's rays traveling to earth, that was credited for life on Earth. Light, heat and sound waves were seen science; the energy carried by the waves was unseen spiritual reproductive, regenerative power of the Creator of all living things. (Prof. Kaba) [see also; "Dark Light Consciousness" by Dr. Edward B. Bynum]

Melanated people were spiritual in ancient times long before religion. We lived by the divine laws of nature. In antiquity, the essence of spirituality was expressed thoroughly throughout our nations. One main Creator (The Universal ALL) with extended attributes such as the sun; the cosmos; the ocean; the land; and even man himself was our understanding of spiritual consciousness. It wasn't until Cultural Imperialism that we began to put our understanding into a **BOX**.

B.) Appearance

Every culture has its own unique way of expressing what their views of beauty are. It's common practice for the invader to change the entire viewpoint of what beauty is. This will cast a certain level of insecurity amongst the people. The cultural clothing, hairstyling, jewelry accessories, body markings, and even genetic features will be frowned upon do to subjective behavior towards a people.

1.) Hairstyle

The melanated culture has always been creative when it comes to hairstyling in particular. The creator blessed us with curly, knotty, crinkly, and wavy hair for a reason. By paying close attention you can see that melanated hair grows upwards towards the Sun and Cosmos (defies gravity). Curly, knotty, and crinkly hair serves as antennas to the Universe which also strengthen our frequency levels. These frequencies are interconnected to each and every cosmic vibrational frequency.

Whenever you get extremely mad or excited about something, have you noticed the hair on your neck and other body parts tend to stand up? It connects us spiritually to everything around us, believe it or not. Consequently, we had to deal with culture vultures who made us think that nappy hair was bad hair and straight hair was good hair. By default, we figured out a way to mix chemicals together while creating the perm for hair straightening. This process made us feel more accepted in society.

Several different hairstyles have been frowned upon through the centuries, particularly by the Christian church. Braided hair is a perfect example of this statement. The Apostle Paul demonized braided hair in the King James version of the Bible. Here are a few Scripture references you can look up for yourself. 1 Timothy 2:9 - reads- *In like manner also, that women adorn themselves in modest apparel, with shamefacedness and sobriety; not with **braided** hair,* or gold, or pearls, or costly arrays. Other scriptures such as 1 Peter 3:3, and 1 Timothy 2:8-15, also speaks against braided hair. Ever ask why they specifically targeted braided hair? Historical evidence reveals that melanated people were the first to braid and twist their hair, so why was it culturally demonized in the Bible? I ask these questions because no logical explanations have been made to justify those texts. You should find it very strange that even in "holy" scriptures we are targeted in some form or another.

To understand certain contradictions and biases in the Bible we must search for the root of the problem. The modern-day version of the Bible that we read today was authorized by a European king by the name of King James I of England (formally King James VI of Scotland). He was the author of a demonic book titled "Daemonologie" in 1597 and was viewed as a troubled intellectual. King James's mother Queen Mary of Scotland was beheaded for treason on February 8, 1587. He calmly agreed to her execution, and upon Queen Elizabeth's death James became king of England, Scotland and Ireland in 1603. In addition to this heinous act, he was also accused of being a homosexual which contradict teachings within the very scriptures he authorized. (Don't misinterpret me as being homophobic, I'm simply explaining some key points.)

In the year 1604 there was a conference of scholars, clergymen and government officials who insisted on a new version of the bible. The new version was requested to have a more political stance on society that governs the people. Nearly fifty scholars were chosen to dissect the previous books; add inserts to several passages; and throw out the ones that were deemed unnecessary. After seven years of reconstructing the bible, King James' new version was authorized in 1611. With so many different modifications that took place over time, how can we not see the underhanded agendas used to manipulate the masses. Research has brought me to the conclusion of realizing that King James was neither mentally nor ethically fit to authorize any spiritual literature for a people.

(Hairstyles of the ancient people in Kemet)

2.) Clothing

I'm a man who enjoys wearing African tribal attire. Dashiki shirts are extremely comfortable and gives me a sense of pride when I wear them. The connected feeling, I receive towards the Motherland is immensely powerful when dressed in African clothing. Oddly enough, I encounter backlash from my own people at times when I wear them. Remarks like "Why you got that African stuff on?" Or "It's not even Black History month yet..." really helps me to understand how lost some melanated people are. Instead of embracing the culture, they prefer to represent the European culture when it comes to attire. Most Africans in America rather pay thousands of dollars on designer clothing just to look like they have money and feel validated by doing so. This type of behavior comes from the obvious brainwashing of colonialism. I'm in no position to dictate how someone spends their own hard-earned money, but certain discussions must be made. The problem comes in when we start to reject our cultural heritage and frown towards its uniqueness.

3.) Accessories and symbols

The **ANKH** cross has been symbolic for eternal life (The Key Of Life) since the beginning of civilization. It is represented in thousands of drawings in the tombs, temples, lodges, and learning centers throughout the ancient Alkebulan (African) world. While studying the symbol you can discover these metaphorical meanings behind it. The top oval part represents the woman's womb. The two sides in the middle represent the woman's ovaries. The bottom section represents the male shaft (penis), or in some interpretations it is the birth canal. As long as these three components come together there will always be eternal **LIFE** through reproduction.

The ankh can also be symbolic to nature as well. The top section is represented by the **Sun**, which brings forth the energy source that sustains life. The two sides are represented as **sunset and sunrise**, which is metaphoric for the cycle of life (birth and death; in humans and plant life). The lower section represents the portal in which **ALL** is resurrected from natural manifestation.

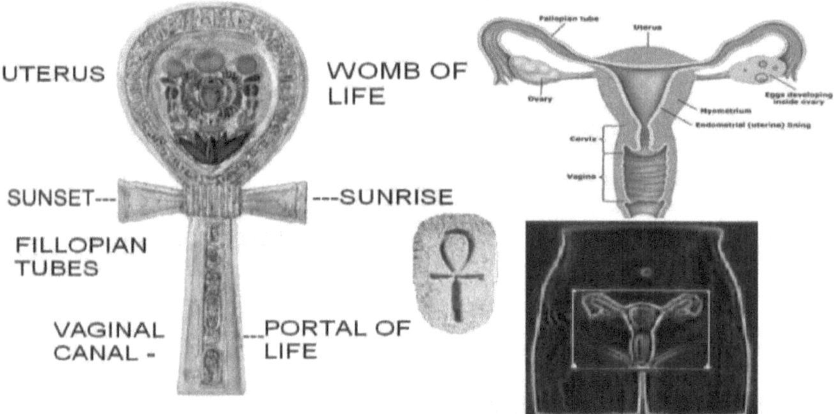
ANKH
The Kemetic Womb of Mankind and Eternal Life
UTERUS
WOMB OF LIFE
SUNSET---
---SUNRISE
FILLOPIAN TUBES
VAGINAL CANAL -
---PORTAL OF LIFE
Fallopian tube
Uterus
Ovary
Eggs developing inside ovary
Myometrium
Endometrial (uterine) lining
Cervix
Vagina
http://amen-parankh.blogspot.com

Different stones, crystals, and precious metals were widely used as spiritual amulets in antiquity by our ancestors. Even in today's time many oracles, priests, and spiritual healers use them for rituals and personal preferences. In the modern era we are taught to view these precious stones and metals as satanic without understanding their true meanings. Here I will name a few of them with their specific qualities.

Lapis Lazuli was a stone highly prized by the ancient Egyptians which dates back to 3100 B.C. It was called the Stone of Rulers which was thought to bring wisdom, truth and insight.

Malachite (Green Stone/Midwife-Stone) was used as a healing stone. It is a powerful healer and balancer on every level, and has natural bacteriostatic qualities, so can be used to support the immune system and fight infection.

Black Tourmaline Stone is used as an energy protector. It absorbs negative energies and disruptive frequencies that is manifested by bad spirits.

Gold (Au) has a unique warm vibrating energy that helps your overall biological and spiritual wellness. It is a natural mineral that possesses a non-toxic infrastructure that reacts great with the human body. Gold also reduces soreness by relaxing blood vessels and allowing blood to flow freely. This process regulates the oxygen in your body. There are other benefits such as Mood Enhancement; Skin Care; Body Temperature Regulation and much more.

Silver (Ag) is an antibacterial mineral which can be transformed into **Colloidal Silver.** Colloidal Silver is a combination of silver particles suspended into a liquid composed mostly of water. In antiquity, colloidal silver was used as an all-purpose medical treatment for diseases, infections and body filtering. It is also said to have the ability to treat HIV/AIDS, tuberculosis and Lyme disease.

Copper (Cu) has great benefits for the human body, especially when combined with iron. Studies have shown that copper helps the body maintain a healthy immune system, bone integrity, healthy blood vessels, and a healthy nervous system. It also helps with arthritis and other illnesses dealing with the human joints and tissue. Antioxidant functions are also found in this precious metal, which reduces the production of free radicals.

The 7 Chakra Stones

The Chakra system is composed of separate energy sources which are aligned inside of the human body. These energies regulate the physical organs, which improves health, strength, and overall wellness. They also ignite the spiritual consciousness that enables the illuminating process for higher-self ascension.

1. The Crown Chakra (**violet**)- The Crown Chakra is associated with the pituitary gland, nervous system, and the brain with its element of light. In its balanced state, this chakra can render individuals the ability to perform miracles, transcend the laws of nature, and have a heightened awareness of death and immortality.

2. The Third Eye Chakra (**indigo**)- This chakra is associated with the chakra color indigo and is connected to the pineal or pituitary gland. Those with a well-balanced Brow or Third Eye Chakra can have telepathic abilities, a charismatic personality and they often do not have any fear of death. The element of electricity or telepathy, along with the chakra color of indigo, are associated with our sense of Thought.

3. The Throat Chakra (**blue**) - As the name suggests, the Throat Chakra with its chakra color blue is associated with the ability to

communicate and listen. The glands to which the Throat Chakra is attached are the esophagus, ears, throat, thyroid, jaws, teeth and neck vertebrae. The ethereal element of the Throat Chakra, when balanced, allows an individual to have a pleasant voice, artistic abilities, expressive ways and also the ability to be in a higher place spiritually. People with a balanced Throat Chakra are able to meditate well and use their energy efficiently and artistically.

4. The Heart Chakra (**green**) - This chakra influences our relationships and is related to the element of air. A weak Heart Chakra is responsible for sabotaging relationships through distrust, anger and envy. Sense of touch is impacted by the Heart Chakra and the glands connected to it are thymus and lymph.

5. The Solar Plexus Chakra (**yellow**) - It is responsible for one's personal and professional success. The chakra color yellow of this energy vortex is associated with fire, energy and charge. This element of fire, when balanced and harmonious, allows one to feel more confident, cheerful and energetic, along with a right amount of respect for self and others. Our sense of sight is associated with the Solar Plexus Chakra. The glands or organs associated with the Solar Plexus Chakra are the adrenal glands.

6. The Sacral Chakra (**orange**) - This Chakra relates to the water element in the human body. The chakra color orange impacts sexuality, reproductive function, joy, desire and even creativity and compassion

for others. The sense of Taste is associated with the Sacral Chakra. Glands and organs impacted by this chakra include the lymphatic system, female reproductive organs, large intestine, pelvis and bladder.

7. The Root Chakra (**red**) - This Chakra defines our relation to Earth. It impacts our vitality, passion and survival instincts. The red chakra color is also indicative of our need for logic and order, physical strength and sexuality, as well as the fight or flight response when faced with danger. The sense of smell in the human body is connected to the Root Chakra. The gland to which the Root Chakra is attached is the gonads.

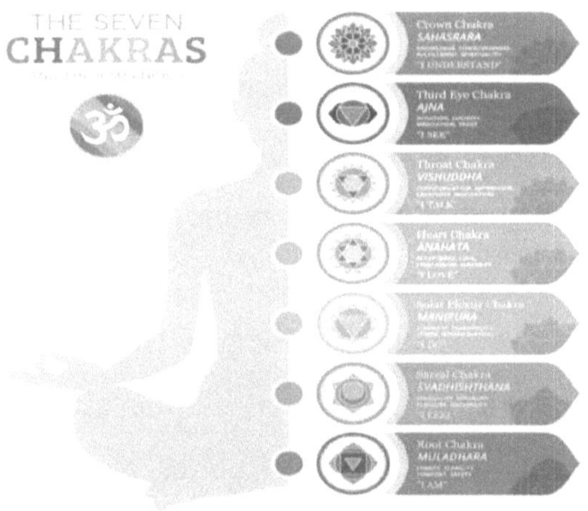

(The 7 Chakras chart; Photo credit, Deposit Photos)

The **cowrie shell** was used as currency by ancient Africans for centuries. It also serves as a popular choice for jewelry and hair accessories. According to the African legends, the cowrie shells represent goddess protection which is highly powerful and is connected with the strength and power of the Ocean.

C.) The Science of Melanin

Referring to the original people of African descent as **melanated people** (carbonated), has been my preferred choice of words because it is scientifically accurate when describing my brothers and sisters. For many years there have been several monikers placed on people of color. We have been called black, negros, coloreds, and famously niggers. Neither of those words can represent us ethnically. Therefore, "melanated people" in my opinion is more appropriate because it's actually scientific. Melanin is a chemical base that has a formula of (C_{18}, H_{10}, N_2, O_4). The main element in melanin is **carbon** (dark matter). Carbon has an atomic number of (6), and is made up of **6** protons, **6** electrons, and **6** neutrons. Melanin controls the pigmentation of a person's skin tone, hair color, and even eye color. It's even found in plants and trees as well. In some circles it's referred to as "the God particle". Studies have proved its importance when dealing with life sustaining benefits. Melanin serves as a natural sunblock from UV rays; regulates biological rhythms; boosts memory; slows aging; boosts immune systems; and much more. Naturally the "melanated people" are the people of the cosmos, so never let anyone degrade you because of your skin tone.

Here is a scientific explanation of melanin in the skin and inner body by Prof. Kaba Hiawatha Kamene. (Spirituality Before Religion)

Eumelanin *is the most abundant type of melanin in the human body. Eumelanin is a dark brown or black pigment. Eumelanin imparts varying shades of brown to hair and skin, with high concentrations found in the skin of darkly pigmented people. More resilient eumelanin's are deposited in hot and humid regions.*

UltraViolet Radiation (UVR) is the type of solar radiation that is of shorter wavelength and therefore greater energy than visible light.

1.) UVR-A -Ultraviolet Radiation of relatively low energy.

2.) UVR-B- Ultraviolet radiation of relatively high energy.

3.) UVR-C- The highest ultraviolet radiation

Mammals in equatorial and tropical regions have a darker skin pigmentation. Absorption of a certain amount of UV radiation is necessary for the production of certain vitamins, notably Vitamin D3. There are four types of Vitamin D, Vitamin D1, D2, D3, and D4. Once impacted by the sun's light, sound and heat energy: D1 and D2 are converted to D3 and D4.

The skin consists of two primary layers: the inner layer called the dermis, composed largely of connective tissue and the outer thinner epidermis. This thickness of the epidermis ranges from 0.003 to 0.024 inches. (Kaba: Spirituality Before Religion)

Neuromelanin (NM) is a dark pigment found in the brain which is structurally related to melanin. It is a polymer of 5,6-dihydroxyindole monomers. Neuromelanin is found in large quantities in catecholaminergic cells of the substantia nigra pars compacta and locus coeruleus, giving a dark color to the structures. The melanin in the brain refines the nervous system in such a way that it reaches other parts of the body most rapidly in Melanated people. Infants with an abundance of melanin tend to sit up, stand, crawl and walk sooner than those who are less melanated. These infants also demonstrate more advanced cognitive skills as well. Studies have also shown that melanated infants have an extremely higher survival rate than non-melanated infants when dealing with prematurity. Neuromelanin also controls the rhythmic functions in humans which aligns them with cosmic frequencies. This is why melanated people tend to have more rhythm while dancing; clapping their hands to a beat; and tone structure while singing. Melanin is the neuro-chemical basis for what is called SOUL in "Black" people. This is how you get the phrases such as "Soul-food" and "Soul-music".

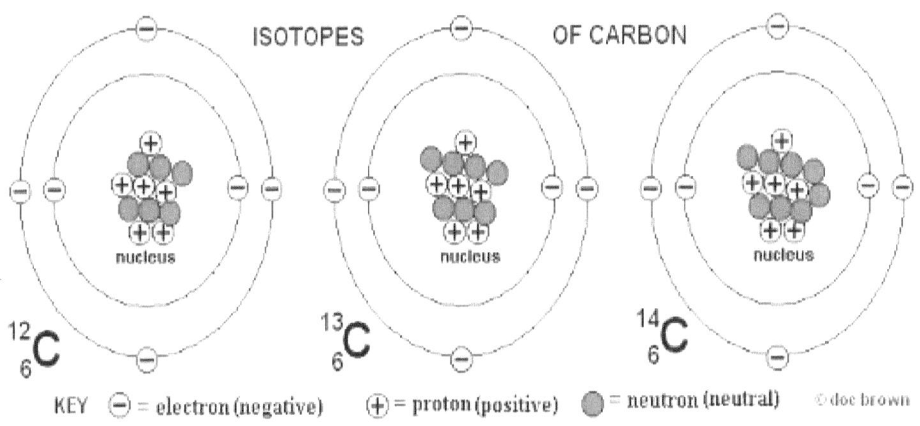

*(6-electron 6-proton 6-neutron = **CARBON** the main elemental makeup of melanin in the Universe; Photo credit, DocBrown)*

D.) Black vs White

The wonderful essence of blackness is the original state of all creation from the cosmos to the creation of the human species. Everything comes from darkness no matter how we decipher it. Before you can have light, you must first have darkness in order for any sort of illustration to be visible. In every creation mythology (story) the narrator always explains how darkness preceded any created element. Blackness is the first and last of what we know as creation, and we must dispel the negative narrative that has been accompanied with the word black.

I will show several negative black phrases compared to its white counterpart.

Black sheep - Is the outcast family member

Black ball- Is the act of refusing to admit someone to membership in an organization

Black market - Is an illegal marketing operation

Black magic - Is seen as witchcraft

Black cat - Is seen as bad luck

Black hearted - Person with evil intent

Black mail - When someone uses information against someone else to gain leverage

-We wear black at a funeral, and we wear white at weddings.

-The white keys on the piano are dominant to the black keys.

- The white cue ball in the game of pool has to knock off every color (race) of balls in order to be victorious. The (black) 8 ball is the final ball that has to be annihilated off the face of the earth (pool table).

-White is considered to be the total opposite when described as a phrase or common thought.

 White lie - Is when you tell a lie that is harmless

White as snow - In religious hymns it means to be purified from sins… "wash me white as snow"...

White light - Is used to describe a person's vision of heaven in a near death experience

-Angels are white and demons are black.

Everything that deals with the color of white is always considered to be pure, while the color black is associated with evil and negativity. We must understand the mind manipulations that colonialism has tricked us with. When viewing the world with an opened third eye you will begin to uncover the clever ideologies that are used against the melanated people of the cosmos.

E.) NIGGER vs Negus

In modern times, over the past 500 plus years the word nigger has been used as a derogatory term towards melanated people. It has degraded and mislabeled our people in the most disrespected way imaginable. The word nigger can be defined as someone who is ignorant, slow to learn, and the unwillingness to better his or her self. With this being said, it should be understood that anyone with those characteristics can be labeled as a "nigger" no matter what race they are. To label someone as the "N" word just because of their pigmentation is actually showing that those who do so are actually the definition of the word.

In more recent times, the black culture has changed the narrative of the word into something positive. It now can be used as a sign of endearment toward a friend or family member by saying "my nigga". Even the spelling has changed from nigger to nigga. Changing a negative into something positive is not uncommon in our societies. Actually, we can go even deeper into mathematical science and understand this principle because if you have two negatives in a multiplication problem it will equal a positive. These are laws of nature that we can understand by using simple observation.

There has been some debate amongst different scholars on whether "nigger" comes from the word "negus" or not. Centuries ago negus was a word used by the Ethiopians to label someone as king or emperor. It was a word of great esteem within the culture of the people. Some scholars argue that the pronunciation of the two words are so similar that Europeans changed the spelling and transformed it's meaning to somthing negative because of racial prejudice. Other studies have shown the "N" word to date back as far as the ancient Kemet (Egyptian) times. It is said that the original spelling was N-G-R because they did not use vowels in those days. The meaning of the word was still the same as the later Ethiopians used referring to kings and emperors. I personally feel that the "N" word has been manipulated to degrade our people just as many other oppressive tools have been. As long as I'm not personally attacked in a racial way by the "N" word, I have no problem with it because I understand its historical past. But I still refuse to let a white person call me a nigger or use the term in front of me no matter how "cool" we are.

F.) SHEEP

Dealing with an imperialist culture you will find an enormous amount of people with the "sheep" mentality. Brainwashing has taught our people to be comfortable with referencing themselves as sheep. It's a psychological tool that religions use to keep the minds of the masses dependent. A sheep needs to be told what to do at all times and it has no self-dependency. Sheep are easily led to wherever the overseer commands it to go. They obviously cannot think for themselves. For example, the so-called sheep dog is trained to corral a herd of sheep while controlling their whereabouts. How can a foreign animal dictate your situation with no logical reason other than to carry out a command from the superior owner? Even if another creature sneak amongst the herd wearing "sheep's clothing" the sheep would not be able to tell the difference and let them live within the herd. The phrase "wolf in sheep's clothing" is very paramount when identifying the root of this problem. We have to stop feeling comfortable with living as sheep. Each and everyone of us are leaders in our own right. The days of being docile most come to an end before it's too late!

G.) The Meek

"The Meek shall inherit the earth" is a widely used phrase throughout several religions and philosophical sectors. In my personal humble opinion, being "meek" is a dangerous idea for anyone who desires to stand up for themselves. The word **meek** is defined as being passive, easily persuaded, prone to being walked over etc. A meek person just goes with the flow of things not wanting to cause controversy by standing on his/her own logical thought. Being humble has little to do with being meek in the real world. Humbling yourself has more to do with understanding that once you've reached a higher level of a certain entity you have to stay grounded by not forgetting where you came from. In other words not getting the big head and thinking you're better than the next person. So in reality you can be humble without being meek. We hear or read about being meek from biblical and ideological teachings then incorporate it into our subconscious without understanding the true meaning of the phrase. We must research everything we choose to believe in because the power of spoken word will resonate in your everyday life.

Part 2.) Regain Self Awareness

Dr. Ray Hagins shows us how self-awareness can only be gained by recovering who you truly are. *"A people who does not know where they come from can never navigate through the state, they are currently in. Therefore, they will continuously be lost in the foreseeable future."*

-Bro. Lyle

Three steps to regain self-awareness

1.) The first thing we must do to recover is admit that we have been programmed through oppressive ideologies. Being ignorant to this fact will only cause you to continue walking in a sleep state. Our people often refuse to accept the fact that colonialism devised a plan to control our minds with great vigor and succeeded in doing so. They'll admit that we were enslaved or indentured servants, but when you talk about mental enslavement, they choose to cancel that out. Until we realize what's going on beyond the physical, we can never ascend to the recovering stage.

2.) Researching and applying historical knowledge to your everyday walk-in life is critical for the recovering process. Mental strength is the cornerstone for building an immunization against brainwashing tactics. Just like any other muscle in your body, the

brain must be trained hard to gain strength and power. "Knowledge is Power...but only if it's **APPLIED**".

3.) We must have unity in the melanated communities at the end of the day. Trying to thrive without love, respect, appreciation and concern for one another is virtually impossible. Denouncing the old "crab in the bucket" mentality is imperative. Melanated people around the world are treated poorly from most races, so what since does it make for us to treat ourselves in such a manner.

Let us **UNITE** with one another so that we can be liberated as a strong people.

"In order to become conscious in your reality you must cleanse yourself of all unnecessary trash within. You cannot heal a cut without first removing the dirt that's underneath the skin's surface. Spreading Neosporin over a dirty cut will ultimately trap the infection.." -Bro. Lyle

(This is a picture of the original Holy Trinity- Father, Mother, and Child; Ancient Kemetic teachings taught this principle as the circle of life and union; The invaders took the female principle out and added the Holy Spirit)

Chapter V. Black Economics

"We the Melanated people, were not born in (sin) like some would say; Most of us are born in (debt), because of generational economic miseducation, undervaluing credit responsibility, and economic exploitation." -Bro. Lyle

Economically empowering the Melanated people is as important as any other topic mentioned in this body of work. What is the most common question mentioned when speaking of breaking free from mental chains? Well, I'll explain what it is. Everyone always asks, "What should we do now?" "What is the final solution after we've marched, protested, and boycotted?" These common questions can be answered with one simple phrase. **"Black Economics!"**

In our communities we have been dealing with gentrification, economic exploitation, and lack of economic education. As children most of us were not taught about how money works. We were taught to go to school in order to receive a degree so that we can work for someone else. Learning how to be financially stable with an entrepreneurship mind set should have been taught instead. Credit was also a part of the mis educational process. Most parents taught their children that credit was something negative or non-essential. Realizing how misinformed our communities are can only help to rectify the problem.

<u>Exploitation</u>

"Being exploited means we are taken advantage of economically by those who know more than us when it comes to money, banking, real estate, stocks, insurance, taxes, entrepreneurship etc." (Jay Morrison: "The Solution")

Melanated people in America spend almost 2 trillion dollars annually in the U.S. with hardly anything to show for it. A simple trip to the "Black" neighborhoods is more than enough evidence to validate this claim. Every major ghetto and housing projects are overpopulated with melanated people. Ask yourself how is this even possible given the fact that we circulated so much money throughout the country.

"If your money doesn't stay home others will prosper from it." -Bro. Lyle

The late great Malcolmn X stated something so profound in his "Ballot or the Bullet" speech that speaks to the "black" dollar. Here's a statement that he said during the speech.

"The economic philosophy of Black Nationalism only means that we have to become involved in a program of re-education, to educate our people on the importance of knowing that when you spend your dollar out of the community in which you live, the community in which you spend your money becomes richer and richer. The community out of which you take your money becomes poorer and poorer." (Malcolm X: The Ballot or the Bullet)

Supporting Black owned businesses has to be more than just buying a t-shirt, sharing Facebook pages or getting your hair styled from a close friend. To have a seat at the **"BIG TABLE"** we must gather all of our resources to create powerful impactful businesses within the communities. Gas stations, grocery stores, banks, law firms and distribution warehouses are businesses that will make a huge impact. The "crab in the bucket" syndrome has to be expelled in order for the community to prosper. Time after time we worry about who's succeeding and who's not instead of building together as a people. Unity is the main ingredient for economic achievements. During ancient times in the Motherland we used to trade across nations with our foreign brothers and sisters. Having compassion with the will to stimulate the economy amongst ourselves was as normal as breathing for us. Getting back to those principles has to start today!

Black Wall Street

Greenwood, Tulsa, Oklahoma in the early 1900s had one of the most successful melanated communities in recent U.S. history. At its height, the business center of the town boasted of various grocery stores, drug stores, nightclubs, churches, banks, funeral homes, restaurants, and hotels. The community was self-sufficient and became the home for many multi-millionaire entrepreneurs. Majority of those businesses were even more prosperous than some inside of the white communities. Sadly, to say, but this wonderful town was tragically burned down because of jealous, racist white people. They were flat out jealous of the magnificent achievements done by the people of Greenwood. This history has been hidden from the masses for years, but it must be taught so that our people can recognize the potential power of the **"Black Dollar"**.

Black Wall Street should not only be a historical event in time, it should also be viewed as a blueprint for economic empowerment. Starting locally in the small urban towns is key. There has to be a foundation first before any structure can be assembled. "Buying back our

Blocks" is the perfect way to get started. It's no secret that other ethnic groups thrive in the black communities whether its real estate, grocery stores, food chains, hair stores, nail shops, gas stations etc. Seeing an Asian person making millions of dollars off melanated hair products always troubled me for some reason. They sell 95% of products which cater to "blacks". They even have our pictures hanging on the windows and throughout their stores. The crazy part of it all is that most of them don't even like us personally. I remember on several different occasions where I would give the cashier money in his hand, but when he would give me my change back he would throw it on the counter even if my hand was open to receive it. Reading how the Chinese treated the Africans in China during the covid-19 pandemic clarifies my point. This is why we cannot continue to let other ethnic groups exploit us economically over and over again. Wake up and build wealth collectively! Stop beating your brother and sister down with negativity. There has to be a time when we support each other unapologetically! If you see your brother with the same hair store as the China man next door, make the conscious decision to support him even if it may cost an extra dollar or two. Remember that he was not given the same extra tax breaks and grants as the China man did, so his prices may have to start off a bit higher at the beginning. More product and demand will eventually reduce the distribution cost and in turn lower the prices.

Gaining economic leverage in communities will also bring in a sense of pride. Financial stability will give the youth a platform to look up to as well. Seeing successful people within their same hue is pivotal for the young developing minds to observe. Children are like sponges and will soak up every visual content that's exposed to them. Learning economical structures as a youth holds great value for our children. Crime rates will eventually decrease drastically throughout the melanated communities because of this fact. Instead of believing that drugs, stealing, prostitution, and other crimes are the only accessible means of income, they will have hope of a better way out **LEGALLY**.

I don't profess to have all the answers, but I do know it starts locally. With every ounce of LOVE in me for my people, I urge you to change the status quo. Let us build together as one for the sake of our future and global stability!

<u>Power of Credit</u>

Credit is widely misunderstood in our communities. We were taught to be afraid of credit instead of embracing it as a tool for financial freedom. In most cases the ones who actually have a pretty good score treat their credit as something sacred and refuse to test the potential business side of it. They're afraid of a few dropped points, and lack the understanding that credit can always be restored and replenished. What sense does it make to have an 800 credit score all your life and never use it to access funds for creating your own business? Studies have shown that most rich people use debt to gain wealth and rarely use their own capital. It's important that we start learning how to use the bank's money to get ahead financially, because opportunity is in abundance. In this day in time, there are various social media platforms that teach about credit and financial literacy. Now is not the time to set back and wait for a lottery miracle or a lawsuit. Start building your credit today at all costs because time waits for no one.

Helpful Credit tips

1.) Keep your credit card usage rate under 20%.

2.) Pay off debt if you can afford to.

3.) Don't close unused credit cards because it will lower your age of credit history.

4.) Dispute inaccurate credit reports by filling yourself or by calling the bureau.

5.) Leverage your personal credit in order to receive business credit.

6.) Don't apply for too much credit at one time this will draw a red flag.

7.) Become an authorized user on someone else credit card who has a good history report and on time payments. They do not have to give you one of their cards. This technique is called Piggybacking, Tradelines, or Authorized user.

8.) Build your child's credit early by letting him/her piggyback off your credit line.

Helpful financial tips to build wealth for the average person

1.) Buy a house and get a 15-year fixed mortgage rather than a 30 year mortgage. It will save you a lot of interest over the lifespan of the loan. If you have to get a 30-year mortgage verify a no prepayment penalty clause. This will give you the flexibility of making lower payments when times get tough.

2.) Try not to buy a car brand new if possible. A 90k dollar vehicle will lose its value in a couple years and be worth 40k while you still owe roughly 75k on it.

3.) Get yourself an LLC (incorporate your name) and run it as a S Corp. This can also help you when tax season comes around.

4.) Build business credit. Business loans are larger and the interest rate will be lower.

5.) Open up a business bank account when you start your business.

6.) Get life insurance (term life and whole life) for you and your children as soon as possible. The sooner you get the insurance the cheaper it will be. You can borrow against it to fund different investments if needed. The ones that pay out dividends are the best.

7.) You can leverage your home to get funding for an investment. The equity that is accumulated in your home is a great way to get going. Choose a HOLEC strategy over the traditional Cash-out-refinancing. With the HOLEC you will use it as a revolving line of credit, which means whatever you take out you can put it back and only pay what you use. Cash-out-refinancing gives you a lump sum amount of cash and you have to start paying it back immediately. (1-6 *Comes from a smart post written by a unanimous social media blogger)*

(Map showing regions of historical massacres of Melanated people)

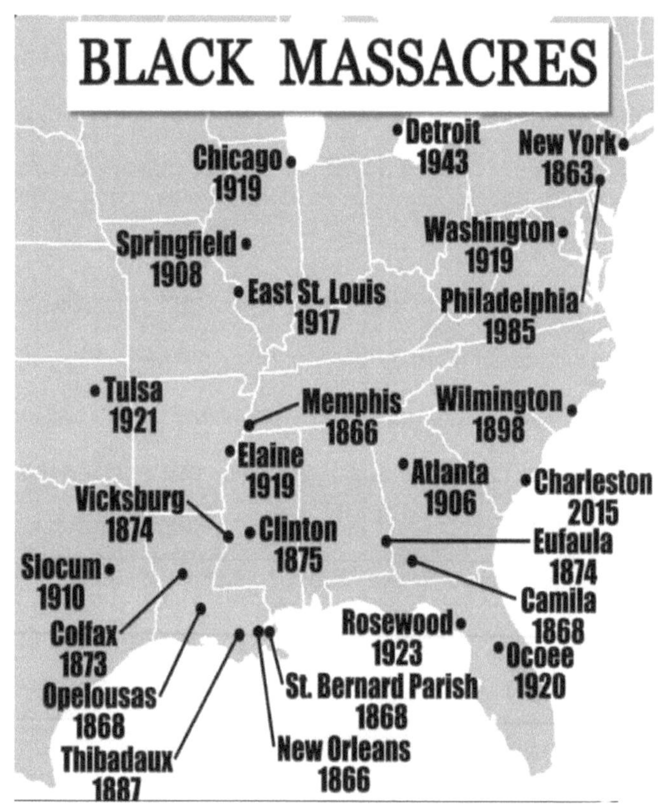

(The Great Black Wall Street; Greenwood, Tulsa Oklahoma 1921; photo credit Tulsa World blog)

(Aftermath of the Black Wall Street Massacre; Tulsa World blog)

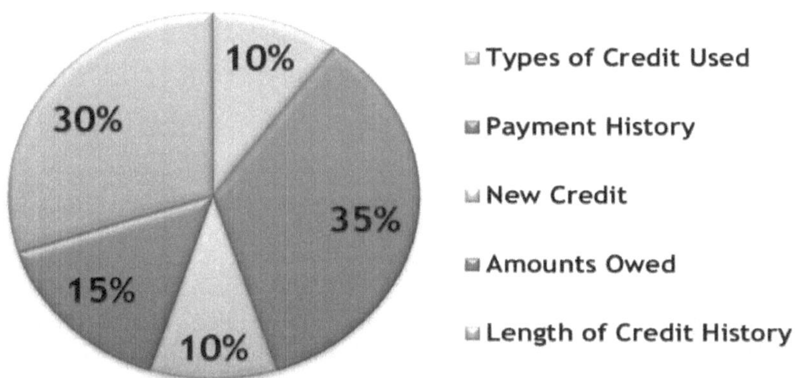

(Credit Chart that shows what dictates your score, photo credit RMS)

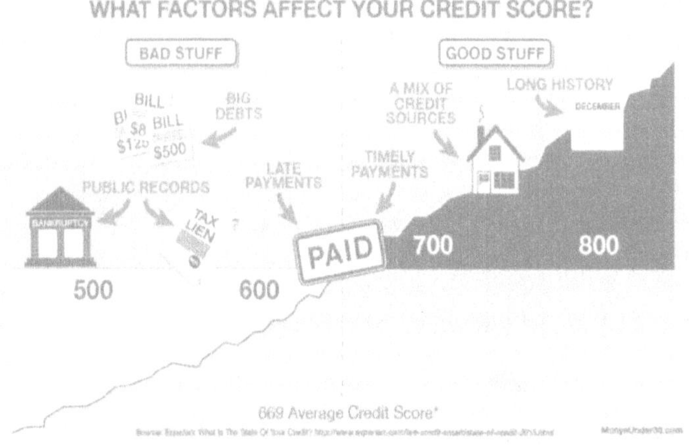

(The factors that affect your credit score; photo cred Trinity KCK)

Chapter VI. Manifest Your Dreams

"To dream of greatness is to envision reachable possibilities, don't let fear of nightmares hinder you from reaching those goals." -Bro. Lyle

Last but definitely not least, we have reached the final step for liberating yourself. After carefully examining each step towards this euphoric experience, it's necessary to capture the ultimate goal. Collapsing every stigma, roadblock, stereotype and systematic oppression has to be rewarded by manifesting your dreams.

Can you imagine a world without that first dreamer? Can you picture billions of people on Earth living with not one evolutional invention? The entire human race would have been on the verge of extension if there was not for those thousands of evolutionary inventions which stems from dreaming. Just think about the early homo-sapien-sapiens who used simple stone and wood for survival tools thousands of years ago. Their imagination enabled them to continue a trend for modernizing early technology throughout the ages. In every aspect of history, there was always that one courageous person who dreamed of a better way. Tracing back as far as ancient times to as recently as today, you can prove this theory.

Given the chance of failure we tend to cast off our dreams. We often use excuses with poor explanations such as, "I don't have the time," "What if I fail?" and "What would others think?" Doubt in human thought processing is completely normal, but you have to trust in the possibility of success.

Windows of opportunities have come and gone since the first sunset of humanity. Those who decided to grab hold with an untying grip were the ones who always excelled in life. By comparison, those who simply gave up at the first sign of trouble prematurely crippled their chances. I was always taught, "in order to get to something you have to go through something." For the dreamer this means he or she has to overcome fear of defeat before the dream is accomplished. By doing so you will begin to climb treacherous mountains with ease. Doors which were once locked will begin to open freely. Every failure would be just another valuable lesson learned that you can carry for the rest of your days.

Underestimating the power of constructive struggles can be an unseen weakness. Adversity almost always builds character and strengthens one's walk in life. You can do all the research in the world and I guarantee not one great dreamer had an easy road. In the event of "short term" failure it's up to you to get back up, dust off, and keep striving. Use those moments to grow stronger by learning from previous mistakes because you must become conscious of every triumph and defeat.

Believing in yourself is the first process you must incorporate in order to be successful. Without truly believing in your vision, there is no possible way you can achieve the task at hand. Please understand that dreams and beliefs feed off one another. Every Super Bowl champ, NBA champ, World Series champ, Boxing champ etc., believed they were going to win since the beginning of the season. I'll bet my bottom dollar that you'll never hear anyone of them speaking of a negative fate. Channeling your thought process to positive thinking will always keep your frequency uplifted.

There may come a time when believing seems to be a waste of time. Everything may appear to always be going against your expectations. Every time you try to carry out a plan something always derails it. I'm here to inform you that even in a perfect world there still may be obstacles that life throws at you. Logically speaking, there's too many variables at play for 7.5 billion people on Earth to have their way all at once. With that being said, you should never blanket your determination no matter what. The laws of reality may suggest that success is a 50/50 chance, but we must believe in the positive portion of the ratio.

Always remember that preparation is essential for every level of success as well. Timely planning and coordinating will come easy by consolidating all accessible information needed to reach a certain goal. Also remember that every great invention came from a previous idea. Every phenomenal leader learned from someone wiser than them. At the end of the day research and resources will always aid you in the preparation phase of any desired goal.

My dear **BEAUTIFUL Melanated People** must understand the importance of this message for manifesting your dreams. We have to rise up and take chances by pursuing every dream and aspirations that our heart desires. Fear of failing must become a thing of the past. No one but yourself can stop you from attaining success, this is why believing in yourself is imperative.

Chapter VII. Great Liberational Quotes and Philosophies

<u>Anthony T. Browder</u>

"The hostility that we exhibit toward each other stems from years of miseducation and unresolved personal conflicts."

"In order for Black people to understand the nature of the world they live in, they must first understand the nature of the people who interpreted the world for them."

"The liberation of the African mind, body, and spirit can only be achieved through the use of an African centered value system that makes the study of the successes and failures of the past the highest priority."

<u>Marcus Garvey</u>

"A people without the knowledge of their past history, origin and culture is like a tree without roots."

"Liberate the minds of men and ultimately you will liberate the bodies of men."

"If you have no confidence in self, you are twice defeated in the race of life."

"Take advantage of every opportunity; where there is none, make it for yourself."

"The Black skin is not a badge of shame, but rather a glorious symbol of national greatness."

<u>Malcolm X</u>

"Nobody can give you freedom. Nobody can give you equality or justice or anything. If you're a man, you take it!"

"Education is the passport to the future, for tomorrow belongs to those who prepare for it today."

"If you're not careful, the newspapers will have you hating the people who are being oppressed and loving the people who are doing the oppressing."

"There can be no Black and White unity until there is first some Black unity. There can be no worker's solidarity until there is first some racial solidarity!"

Booker T. Washington

"In all things that are purely social we can be as separate as the fingers, yet one as the hand in all things essential to mutual progress."

"Success is to be measured not so much by the position that one has reached in life as by the obstacles which he has overcome."

John Henerik Clarke

"History is not everything, but it is a starting point. History is a clock that people use to tell their political and cultural time of day. It is a compass they use to find themselves on the map of human geography. It tells them where they are, but more importantly, what they must be."

"Powerful people cannot afford to educate the people that they oppress. Because once you are truly educated you will not ask for power, You will take it."

"Racists will always call you a racist when you identify their racism. To love yourself now is a form of racism. We are the only people criticized for loving ourselves, and white people think when you love yourself you hate them. No, when I love myself they become irrelevant to me."

Dr. Yosef Ben Jochannan

"Truth is a continuous examination, and fact always supersedes belief."

"When your god and your savior looks like your master and enslaver, you become the principal agent in your destruction."

Dr. Leonard Jefries

"Whoever controls the images, controls your self-esteem, self-respect and self-development. Whoever controls the history controls the vision."

Dr. Martin Luther King Jr.

"Darkness cannot drive out darkness, only light can do that." Hate

cannot drive out hate, only love can do that.”

“In the end, we will remember not the words of our enemies, but the silence of our friends.”

Dr. Ray Hagins

“Whoever controls the printed page controls the thinking of the age.”

“The space inside this circle represents my realm of knowledge. All that I think I know about whatever I think I know is depicted right here within this circle! I must keep in mind that there is more to know than what is within the circumference of my awareness.”

Prof. Kaba Hiawatha Kamene

“The future depends on what you do in the present.”

"If they don't change their ways, The Way is going to change them. Nature never takes anyone's side. Nature takes its OWN side and acts when it's the natural time."

"It ain't over until we win"; "Keep on keeping on"

<u>Jay Morrison</u>

"Wealth is not about how much money you make, but how much you keep."

"We think it's the respect of others that we want, but it's the respect of ourselves that we need."

"Business is formalized hustle; Hustle is informal business."

<u>Cheikh Anta Diop</u>

"Intellectuals ought to study the past not for the pleasure they find in so doing, but to derive lessons from it."

"Only a loyal, determined struggle to destroy cultural aggression and bring out the truth, whatever it may be, is revolutionary and consonant with real progress; it is the only approach which opens onto the universe. Humanitarian declarations are not called for and add nothing to real progress."

Bob Marley

"Emancipate yourself from mental slavery none but ourselves can free our minds, have no fear for atomic energy cause none of them can stop the time."

James Baldwin

"Not everything that is faced can be changed; but nothing can be changed until it is faced."

"To be a Negro in the country and to be relatively conscious is to be in a rage almost all the time."

"We can disagree and still love each other, unless your disagreement is rooted in my oppression and denial of my humanity and right to exist."

<u>Thomas Sankara</u>

"Imperialism is a system of exploitation that occurs not only in the brutal form of those who come with guns to conquer territory…"

"We are fighting this system that allows a handful of men on earth to rule all of humanity."

"Knowledge is not enough to change the conditions of Black people. Understand that we need to create programs and systems that will empower us economically, spiritually, and mentally. We need courage and action."

Frederick Douglass

"Knowledge makes a man unfit to be a slave"

"It is easier to build strong children than to repair broken men."

"Find out what people will submit to, and you have found out the exact amount of injustice and wrong which will be imposed on them."

Bro. Lyle

"Don't let the colonizers tell you what the truth is. Read, research, investigate and think for yourself. Every aspect of existence is always deeper than the surface."

"To gain leverage on life you must first possess a conscious balance within."

"If the root of a tree is artificial, how can you expect it to produce real fruit?"

"I'm not sorry for believing in my own natural reasoning. I'm not sorry for not allowing you to interpret to me what you perceive to be true. I'm not sorry for questioning that which I believe should be questioned."

"A people who does not know where they come from can never navigate through the present state they are in and in turn will continually be lost in the future."

"Be strong in a weak world, seek knowledge in a lost world, then you can wake up in a sleeping world; understand who you are first before understanding the complexity of the world."

"In order to become conscious in your reality you must cleanse yourself of all unnecessary trash within. You cannot heal a cut without first removing the dirt that's underneath the skin's surface. Spreading Neosporin over a dirty cut will ultimately trap the infection."

"We the Melanated people were not born in (sin) as the religious groups like to say. We are born in (debt), because of generational economic miseducation, undervaluing credit responsibility, and economic exploitation."

"We can never CHANGE the past; but we can always REVOLUTIONIZE the future…"

Bibliography

Allah, C'CS Alife & Understanding, Supreme: The *Science of Self; Man, God, and the Mathematical Language of Nature (Supreme Design, LLC; 3rd Edition, June 6, 2012)*

Allen, James : *As A Man Thinketh (Jeremy P Tarcher, January 1, 2008)*

Bynum, Edward B. : *Dark Light Consciousness; Melanin, Serpent Power, and the Luminos Matrix of Reality (Inner Traditions, 2012)*

Chandler, Wayne B. :*Ancient Future (Black Classic Press, 1999)*

Diop, Cheikh Anta : *The African Origin of Civilization; Myth or Reality (Independent Publishers Group, 1974)*

Dubois, Laurent : *Avengers of The New World; The Story of the Haitian Revolution (The Belknap Press, Oct. 31, 2005)*

DuBois, W.E.B. : *The Souls Of Black Folk (Dover Publications, Inc, Unabridged Edition, July 14, 2016)*

Garvey, Amy : *Philosophy And Opinions of Marcus Garvey (Martino Fine Books, November 19, 2014)*

James, George G.M. : *Stolen Legacy; Greek Philosophy is Stolen Egyptian Philosophy (Published; 1954)*

Kamene, Kaba Hiawatha : *Spirituality Before Religions; Spirituality is Unseen Science…Science is Seen Spirituality (Independently Published July 22, 2019)*

Kiros, Teodros : *Zara Yacob; Rationality of the Human Heart (Publishers and Distributors of Third World Books, 2005)*

Lama, Dalai : *How to Practice the Way; The way to a Meaningful Life (Atri Books, August 19, 2003)*

Morrison, Jay : *The Solution; How Africans in America Achieve Unity, Justice and Repair (Good2Go Publishing, Oct. 1, 2016)*

Schrijver, Karel : *Living With The Stars; How the Human Body is Connected to the Life Cycles of the Earth, the Planets, and the Stars (Oxford University Press, March 17, 2019) [Reprint Edition]*

Scranton, Laird : *Sacred Symbols of The Dogon; The Key to Advanced Science in the Ancient Egyptian Hieroglyphs (Inner Traditions, October 12, 2007)*

Sertima, Ivan Van : *They Came Before Columbus; The African Presence In Ancient America (The Random House Publishing Group, 1976)*

Shabazz, Allen J. Z. : *Black History In A Nutshell (MPC Publishers January 1, 2013)*

Steiner, Rudolf *: Knowledge Of The Higher Worlds And Its Attainment; On Consciousness, Dream Life And Initiation (Create Space Independent Publishing Platform, September 9, 2014)*

Three Initiates *: The Kybalion: Century Edition (TeachersPerigee, Centennial Edition, January 30, 2018)*

Williams, Chancellor *: Destruction of Black Civilization; Great Issues of Race From 4,500 B.C.E to 2000 A.D (Published by Third World Press 1974, 1987)*

Great Starter Books for Research

1. **"Stolen Legacy"** by George G.M. James

2. **"Black History in A Nutshell"** by Allen J.Z. Shabazz

3. **"Ancient Future"** by Wayne B. Chandler

4. **"Destruction of Black Civilization; Great Issues of Race from 4500 B.C.E to 2000 A.D"** by Chancellor Williams

5. **"When the World Was Black"** by Supreme Understanding

6. **"Spirituality Before Religion"** by Prof. Kaba Hiawatha Kamene

7. **"They Came Before Columbus"** by Ivan Van Sertima

8. **"From The Browder File"** by Anthony T. Browder

About the Author

Bro. Lyle is what we call in modern terms, a "Street Scholar". With over a decade of studying Pan African ideology; Philosophy; Psychological Behavior; Metaphysics; and Financial Literacy, he's able to translate his studies into literature for others to learn from. Bro. Lyle is also a spoken word poet who uses his unique, smooth, and charismatic delivery to teach knowledge through poetry. In 2021, he received his spirituality coaching certification. "Self-Liberation For The Melanated People" is Bro. Lyle's first official body of work. With sound scholarship and the desire to help others, Bro. Lyle will soon become a well-respected household name within the conscious community.

Bro. Lyle

www.ingramcontent.com/pod-product-compliance
Lightning Source LLC
Chambersburg PA
CBHW051056250726
48656CB00001B/322